USGBC LEED AP Interior Design + Construction Study Guide

Copyright

Disclaimer

U.S. Green Building Council

2101 L Street, NW
Suite 500
Washington, DC 20037

Trademark

USGBC LEED AP Interior Design + Construction Study Guide Acknowledgments:
The USGBC LEED AP Interior Design + Construction Study Guide is a valuable tool for exam candidates planning to attain the ID+C Specialty. We would like to extend our deepest gratitude to those involved in the production of this resource.

PROJECT TEAM

Green Building Services, Inc. (GBS)
Beth Shuck, *Content Developer*
Caitlin Francis, *Project Manager and Content Developer*
Glen Phillips, *Technical Specialist and Content Developer*
Katrina Shum Miller, *Principal in Charge*
Nina Tallering, *Content Developer*

Institute for the Built Environment (IBE)
Brian Dunbar, *Educational Consultant*
Josie Plaut, *Educational Consultant*

NonObvious Solutions
Elizabeth Gast, *Technical Illustrator and Graphic Designer*
Eric von Schrader, *Instructional Designer*

Prometric
Examination Question Writing Training

LEED Curriculum Committee Members
Draft reviews

USGBC Staff
Karol Kaiser, *Director of Education Development*
Jacob Robinson, *Project Manager*

MATERIALS AND RESOURCES

INDOOR ENVIRONMENTAL QUALITY

INNOVATION IN DESIGN & REGIONAL PRIORITY

APPENDIX

CREDENTIAL OVERVIEW

Congratulations on your decision to pursue the LEED Accredited Professional (AP) Interior Design + Construction credential. You are positioning yourself within the marketplace as a professional who is committed to keeping up with current trends and best practices.

As you prepare for the exam, you will be taking what you already know about LEED and green building and developing greater proficiency in an area that is specific and relevant to your line of work.

Accreditation will certify that you have the knowledge and skills necessary to participate in the LEED application and certification process, hold a firm understanding of green building practices and principles, and are familiar with LEED requirements, resources, and processes.

Best of luck on the exam!

GETTING STARTED ON YOUR LEED AP ID+C CREDENTIAL

Earning the LEED AP ID+C credential requires passing a two-part exam:

PART 1: (Also see the Green Associate credential) A two-hour exam. Passing Part 1 attests to the candidate's general knowledge of green building practices for both commercial and residential spaces and both new construction and existing buildings as well as how to support other professionals working on LEED projects. *If you are a LEED AP without specialty or you have already earned the Green Associate credential, you need to take only Part 2 of the LEED AP ID+C exam. (Go to the Green Building Certification Institute [GBCI] website, www.gbci.org, for details.)* [1]

PART 2: A two-hour exam. Passing Part 2 attests that the individual possesses the knowledge and skills necessary to participate in the design process, to support and encourage integrated design, and to streamline the application and certification process.[2]

You must pass Part 1 before you can take Part 2. You may take both parts of the exam either on the same day or on separate days.

STEP 1: **Read** the GBCI LEED AP Interior Design + Construction Candidate Handbook at www.gbci.org to determine whether you meet the eligibility requirements.

STEP 2: **Register** for and schedule your exam.

Tips: Register in the EXACT name that appears on your I.D. card, and keep your confirmation number.

STEP 3: **Access** the appropriate reference documents.

The LEED® AP Interior Design + Construction Candidate Handbook lists the references that are the sources for exam questions. Some references are available for free download at www.gbci.org, and others can be purchased at www.usgbc.org.

Note that exam reference documents are subject to change as the GBCI exams evolve. Always check the candidate handbooks for the most up-to-date list of reference documents.

Exam Part 1 (Green Associate):

Review the references listed in the LEED AP Interior Design + Construction Candidate Handbook and consider purchasing the Green Building and LEED Core Concepts Guide from the U.S. Green Building Council (USGBC). This core resource is now packaged to include the Study Guide for LEED Green Associate!

---

1   *LEED AP Interior Design + Construction Candidate Handbook* (GBCI, 2009)
2   *LEED AP Interior Design + Construction Candidate Handbook* (GBCI, 2009)

Exam Part 2 (Interior Design + Construction):

References: Examination items are developed from these resources.

- *LEED Reference Guide for Green Interior Design & and Construction Reference Guide*, U.S. Green Building Council (available for purchase at www.usgbc.org/store > Publications);

- *Sustainable Building Technical Manual: Part II*, by Anthony Bernheim and William Reed, (1996);

- *Guidance on Innovation & Design (ID) Credits* (U.S. Green Building Council, 2004);

- *Guidelines for CIR Customers* (U.S. Green Building Council, 2007);

- *LEED Online — Sample Credit Templates* (www.usgbc.org); and

- *Cost of Green Revisited,* by Davis Langdon (2007).

You should be familiar with the content of the U.S. Green Building Council's website, www.usgbc.org, and the Green Building Certification Institute's website, www.gbci.org, including, but not limited to, the various LEED rating systems, LEED checklists, LEED Project Registration, LEED Certification content, and the purpose of LEED Online.

STEP 4: **Start studying!**

Have all of the reference documents available as you work through this study guide, most importantly the LEED Reference Guide for Green Interior Design and Construction.

LEED AP INTERIOR
DESIGN + CONSTRUCTION

I. Content Areas

The exam has seven major areas of focus, which are called out in the candidate handbook. Here is how they align with the Rating System credit categories:

GBCI EXAM AREAS OF FOCUS		LEED RATING SYSTEM CREDIT CATEGORIES
I. Project Site Factors	=	Sustainable Sites (SS)
II. Water Management	=	Water Efficiency (WE)
III. Project Systems and Energy Impacts	=	Energy and Atmosphere (EA)
IV. Acquisition, Installation, and Management of Project Materials	=	Materials and Resources (MR)
V. Improvements to the Indoor Environment	=	Indoor Environmental Quality (IEQ)
VI. Stakeholder Involvement in Innovation	=	Innovation in Design (ID) & Regional Priority (RP)
VII. Project Surroundings and Public Outreach	=	

II. Exam Questions

GBCI exam questions are:

- Developed and validated by global work groups of subject matter experts;
- Referenced to current standards and resources;
- Developed and monitored through psychometric analysis; and
- Designed to satisfy the test development specifications of a job analysis.

The questions assess your knowledge at three levels:

- **Recall questions** test your direct knowledge of concepts. This section may require you to define terms or concepts, recall facts, recognize or identify components or steps in a process, and group items into categories.

- **Application questions** evaluate your knowledge of procedures and performance and may require you to demonstrate how things work, perform calculations following a formula, place components or steps into proper sequence, describe how a process works, and apply a known process or sequence of actions to accomplish a task (such as troubleshooting a problem using a detailed checklist).

- **Analysis questions** test your reasoning and problem-solving abilities. Such questions may require you to demonstrate an understanding of how things work, cause and effect, and underlying rationale; analyze problems and devise appropriate solutions; build a conceptual model of a process; and troubleshoot a problem without a checklist.

Questions follow consistent formats:

- You will likely **never** see an "all of the above," "none of the above," "true/false" or "what is the best?" type of question on this test, because:
    - These questions can cause confusion and have overlapping answers;
    - The test is intended to be clear and straightforward; and
    - The question language is never intended to be tricky.

- You will likely **never** see a credit number listed by itself; any direct reference to a LEED credit will include the full credit name.

- Most acronyms are spelled out so that you do not need to memorize all acronyms you learn.
    - Commonly referenced acronyms may be used (i.e. LEED, ASHRAE, and VOC), so it is still a good idea to know what these acronyms stand for!

- You **will** see some questions with multiple correct answers (for example, a question prompting the reader to "select two" responses).

- While this is not a math test, you **will** need to have a good understanding of the required calculations and equations associated with compliance to LEED prerequisites and credits. The Prometric center will have a built-in calculator on the computer screen for you to use during the exam. No outside calculators will be permitted.

PRACTICE QUESTIONS IN THIS STUDY GUIDE

Practice questions in this guide were written by subject matter experts who were trained by Prometric, which is the same testing company that administers the GBCI LEED exams, using the same guidelines as the item writers for the actual examinations. The practice questions in this guide will help you become familiar with the exam expectations, format, and question type. This should improve your testing skills and alleviate stress on test day, allowing you to focus on core information.

STUDY TIPS

You will learn best if you establish a regular study schedule over a period of time. Daily studying in shorter sessions is more effective for most people than "cramming" in long sessions at the last minute.

Studying with a partner or a group can help you stay on schedule and give you opportunities to quiz and drill with each other.

Here's a step-by-step approach for using your study resources:

- Read the corresponding section in this study guide.

- Take notes and highlight key points.

- Review other reference materials that apply to the category, such as referenced standards, resources listed in the LEED Reference Guide for Green Building Design and Construction, and other ancillary references listed in the LEED AP Interior Design + Construction Candidate Handbook.

- Reread the reference guide categories.

- Use the review questions, learning activities, and practice questions in this guide.

- Continue reviewing and rereading until you are confident you know the material. Flash cards can also help instill confidence, through repetition.

- If there are subject areas with which you are unfamiliar, ask an expert in these areas to explain the concepts and subtopics to you.

EXAM DAY TIPS

General Strategies

- Always arrive early and take a moment to relax and reduce your anxiety.
  - This brief time period will boost your confidence.
  - Use this time to focus your mind and think positive thoughts.
- Plan how you will use the allotted time.
  - Estimate how many minutes you will need to finish each test section.
  - Determine a pace that will ensure that you complete the whole test on time.
  - Don't spend too much time on each question.
- Maintain a positive attitude.
  - Don't let more difficult questions raise your anxiety and steal your valuable time. Move on and find success with other questions.
  - Avoid watching for patterns. Noticing that the last four answers are "c" is not a good reason to stop, go back, and break concentration.
- Rely on your first impressions.
  - The answer that comes to mind first is often correct.
  - Nervously reviewing questions and changing answers can do more harm than good.
  - Use the "marked question" option to mark those questions you are certain that you want to reconsider.
- Plan to finish early and have time for review.
  - Return to difficult questions you marked for review.
  - Make sure you answered all questions.

Multiple Choice Strategies

- Formulate your own answer before reading the options.
  - Look away from the question and see whether you can answer it without looking at the choices. Focus on finding an answer without the help of the alternative options.
- Read all the choices before choosing your answer.
- Eliminate unlikely answers first.
  - Eliminating two alternatives quickly may increase your probability to 50-50 or better.

- Look for any factor that will make a statement false.

  - It is easy for the examiner to add a false part to an otherwise true statement.
  - Test takers often read the question and see some truth and quickly assume that the entire statement is true. For example, "Water boils at 212 degrees in Denver." Water does boil at 212 degrees, but not at Denver's altitude.

- Beware that similar answers provide a clue. One of them is correct; the others are disguised.

  - This is likely not a trick, but make sure you know the exact content being asked.

- Consider the answers carefully. If more than one answer seems correct for a single-answer question:

  - Ask yourself whether the answer you're considering completely addresses the question.
  - If the answer is only partly true or is true only under certain narrow conditions, it's probably not the right answer.
  - If you have to make a significant assumption in order for the answer to be true, ask yourself whether this assumption is obvious enough that everyone would make it. If it is not, ignore that answer.

- If you suspect that a question is a trick question, make sure you're not reading too much into the question, and try to avoid imagining detailed scenarios in which the answer could be true. In most cases, "trick questions" are only tricky because they're not taken at face value.

  - The test questions will include only relevant content and are not intended to trick you or test your reading ability.

INTERIOR DESIGN + CONSTRUCTION

THE RUNDOWN

The LEED for Commercial Interiors Rating System empowers tenants and designers to maximize the potential of the workplace. The rating system provides a set of performance standards for certifying the design and construction of commercial or institutional tenant build-outs of all sizes, both public and private. It is the recognized system for certifying high-performance green interiors that are healthy, productive places to work; are less costly to operate and maintain; and have a reduced environmental footprint. LEED for Commercial Interiors gives the power to make sustainable choices to tenants and designers, who do not always have control over whole-building operations.

Many types of spaces can be certified through LEED for Commercial Interiors, including the following:

- Banks;
- Corporate offices;
- Law firms;
- Showrooms;
- Arts centers;
- Retail stores;
- Government offices;
- Restaurants;
- University buildings;
- Libraries;
- Medical facilities; and
- Design offices.

ID+C	SS	WE	EA	MR	IEQ	IO	RP	Total
Prerequisites	-	1	3	1	2	-	-	**8**
Credits	14	1	6	8	15	2	1	**49**
Possible Points	21	11	37	14	17	6	4	**110**

THE PROCESS AND PLAYERS

The best way to begin the process of seeking LEED for Commercial Interiors certification is to engage the entire project team in a goal-setting charrette to establish sustainability goals for the project. This should take place as early in the design process as possible. Charrette facilitators may follow the Environmental Design Guidelines described in the Sustainable Building Technical Manual: Part II, by Anthony Bernheim and William Reed (Public Technology, Inc. and U.S. Green Building Council, 1996):

- Establish a vision statement that embraces sustainable principles and an integrated design approach.
- Establish the project's green building goals, developed from the vision statement.
- Establish green design criteria.
- Set priorities for the project design criteria.

Once the goals and criteria are established, it is critical to understand the phases and tasks involved in the LEED certification process.

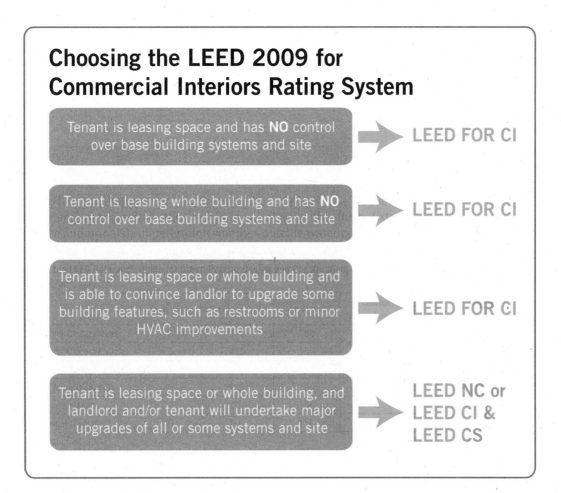

Choosing the LEED 2009 for Commercial Interiors Rating System

Tenant is leasing space and has **NO** control over base building systems and site	→	LEED FOR CI
Tenant is leasing whole building and has **NO** control over base building systems and site	→	LEED FOR CI
Tenant is leasing space or whole building and is able to convince landlor to upgrade some building features, such as restrooms or minor HVAC improvements	→	LEED FOR CI
Tenant is leasing space or whole building, and landlord and/or tenant will undertake major upgrades of all or some systems and site	→	LEED NC or LEED CI & LEED CS

TIME LINE AND TEAM

Achieving LEED certification requires the involvement of the right project team members in each project phase and task.

A time line/team graphic can be found on each credit page that identifies the primary phase and responsible party or parties associated with that prerequisite or credit.

The key phases are as follows:

- Predesign;
- Design;
- Construction; and
- Occupancy.

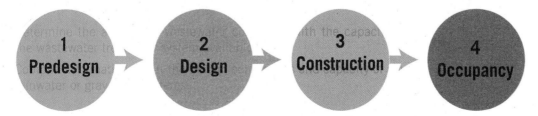

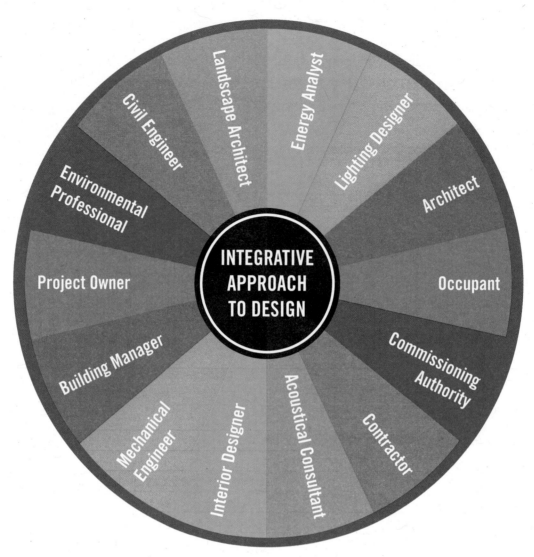

The key players are the following:

- Project owner;
- Occupant;
- Building manager;
- Architect;
- Mechanical engineer;
- Lighting designer;
- Contractor;
- Civil engineer;
- Landscape architect;
- Interior designer;
- Energy analyst;
- Commissioning authority;
- Environmental professional; and
- Acoustical consultant.

An integrative, multidisciplinary approach allows experts to share their knowledge and successfully coordinate individual design efforts to achieve a well-functioning, environmentally responsible, integrated building.[3]

3 *Sustainable Building Technical Manual: Part II*, by Anthony Bernheim and William Reed, (1996)

THE OTHER PARTICULARS

There are other basic elements involved in LEED for Commercial Interiors certification that aren't addressed in any one specific credit, but are integral to the entire rating system. These include the following:

Minimum Program Requirements (MPRs):

Pretty plain and simple - if a project doesn't meet the MPRs, it's not eligible for LEED certification. And, if GBCI learns of non-compliance to the MPRs sometime down the road, they can revoke your LEED certification at any time. Bottom line, become familiar with these basic project requirements and know that they determine project eligibility for LEED. The MPRs will evolve over time and can be found published on the USGBC website at http://www.usgbc.org/DisplayPage.aspx?CMSPageID=2014.

General Submittal Requirements:

The General Submittal Template asks for basic building information and must be completed and uploaded to LEED Online. This template, which also requires the uploading of basic building documents, drawings, and plans, must be consistent across all submitted documentation.

Full-Time Equivalent (FTE):

It is important to establish the occupancy demands on a project early, because this number will affect the approach taken on some LEED prerequisites and credits and should be used consistently in LEED documentation. Calculate the FTE for both full-time and part-time employees, assuming that an 8-hour occupant has an FTE value of 1.0; part-time occupants have an FTE value based on their hours per day divided by the standard occupancy period (typically 8 hours).

$$\text{FTE Occupants} = \frac{\text{Occupant Hours}}{8}$$

Credit Interpretation Requests and Rulings (CIRs):

CIRs were established for project applicants seeking technical and administrative guidance on how LEED credits apply to their projects and vice versa. It is important for project teams to be aware of previous CIRs, as the project must adhere to the CIRs current at the time of registration in addition to the ruling received for their own CIRs. CIRs must be formally submitted online.

Here's what you need to know about CIRs:

- Do your homework! Critically review the intent of the credit/prerequisite and determine whether you are meeting that intent. Consult all available resources, such as the LEED reference guide and previous CIRs, and contact a LEED customer service representative to confirm that your situation warrants a new CIR.

- Properly submit your CIR! Do not include unnecessary or confidential information; provide only what is essential. Request guidance on only one credit or prerequisite, with pertinent background information limited to 600 words. No attachments are accepted!

- There is no guarantee! CIRs do not guarantee a credit award, and you will still have to demonstrate and document achievement during the certification process.

SUSTAINABLE SITES

The project site quite literally and figuratively serves as the foundation for green buildings. Buildings do not exist in a vacuum; they are living parts of a larger fabric, each within its own unique context. The Sustainable Sites (SS) category focuses on selecting sites that reduce dependency on automobiles, incorporating strategies that enhance plant and wildlife habitats, and maintaining water and air quality.

WHAT ABOUT SUSTAINABLE SITES?

What amenities can be provided to encourage carpooling at sites without good access to public transportation?

What design strategies would enhance nighttime security without adding electric lighting?

What environmental implications are associated with the heat island effect? Is the heat island effect a consideration only in urban areas?

What can be done to channel development to urban areas with existing infrastructure?

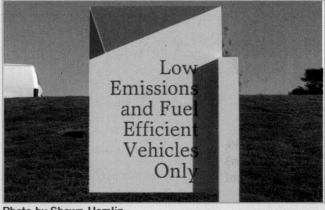

Photo by Shawn Hamlin

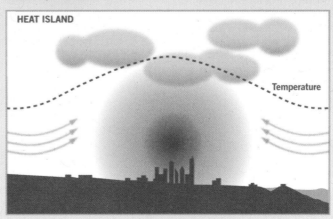

SUSTAINABLE SITES

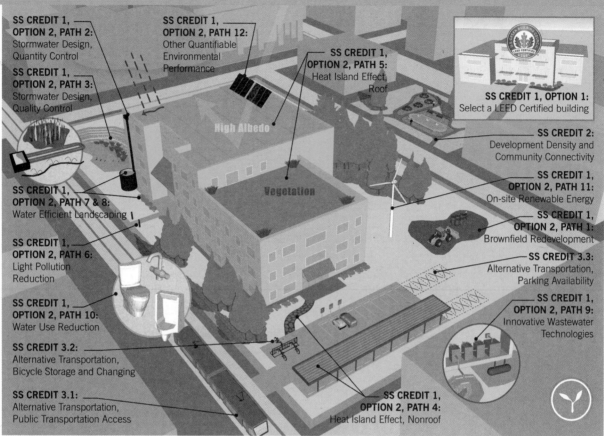

SS CREDIT 1, OPTION 2, PATH 2: Stormwater Design, Quantity Control

SS CREDIT 1, OPTION 2, PATH 3: Stormwater Design, Quality Control

SS CREDIT 1, OPTION 2, PATH 7 & 8: Water Efficient Landscaping

SS CREDIT 1, OPTION 2, PATH 6: Light Pollution Reduction

SS CREDIT 1, OPTION 2, PATH 10: Water Use Reduction

SS CREDIT 3.2: Alternative Transportation, Bicycle Storage and Changing

SS CREDIT 3.1: Alternative Transportation, Public Transportation Access

SS CREDIT 1, OPTION 2, PATH 12: Other Quantifiable Environmental Performance

SS CREDIT 1, OPTION 2, PATH 5: Heat Island Effect, Roof

High Albedo

Vegetation

SS CREDIT 1, OPTION 1: Select a LEED Certified building

SS CREDIT 2: Development Density and Community Connectivity

SS CREDIT 1, OPTION 2, PATH 11: On-site Renewable Energy

SS CREDIT 1, OPTION 2, PATH 1: Brownfield Redevelopment

SS CREDIT 3.3: Alternative Transportation, Parking Availability

SS CREDIT 1, OPTION 2, PATH 9: Innovative Wastewater Technologies

SS CREDIT 1, OPTION 2, PATH 4: Heat Island Effect, Nonroof

OVERVIEW

LEED for Commercial Interiors gives preference to buildings that enhance existing neighborhoods and make use of existing transportation networks and urban infrastructure. The SS credits reward project teams that select buildings that reduce their environmental impact through the following measures:

- Developing the site wisely;
- Incorporating sustainable landscapes;
- Protecting wildlife habitats;
- Managing stormwater runoff;
- Reducing heat island effects;
- Reducing light pollution;
- Incorporating water-efficient landscaping;
- Producing renewable energy on-site;
- Reducing potable water consumption; and
- Reducing emissions associated with transportation.

SUSTAINABLE SITES

SYNERGIES

The Sustainable Sites category has synergies with almost all of the other Commercial Interiors categories because a project's location and site development are intrinsic to the building's ultimate function. In fact, 45% of all credits in LEED for Commercial Interiors are affected by site and building selection. Commercial Interiors projects have the unique ability to add elements to their base building that reduce vehicle travel and improve the surrounding habitat. These attributes also have synergies with the Water Efficiency and Energy and Atmosphere categories to help project teams save resources and reduce operating costs.

One of the most recognizable connections between category components is that between stormwater design and water efficiency. Landscapes that use drought-tolerant and adapted plants not only help slow and filter stormwater but also reduce the need for irrigation—one of the largest uses of water in buildings. Additionally, site development strategies interact with each other. A site with appropriate vegetative features will allow for the allocation of green spaces, as well as assist in stormwater retention and a reduction in the urban heat island effect. Also think about how the building's orientation can affect its energy performance or how selecting a site with ample access to natural resources might influence how far materials have to travel to get to the site.

CATEGORY HIGHLIGHTS

- The Sustainable Sites category offers the most possible points after the Energy and Atmosphere category, with 21 possible points.
- Projects can earn 5 points by locating tenant space in a building that has a LEED certification.
- Know your full-time equivalent (FTE) occupancy for the project in order to complete calculations for several credits. This measure considers all the building users and how many hours they occupy the building. The FTE needs to be used consistently across all credits.

SUSTAINABLE SITES CREDITS

SUSTAINABLE SITE CREDITS

SS

CREDIT	TITLE
SS Credit 1	Site Selection
SS Credit 2	Development Density and Community Connectivity
SS Credit 3.1	Alternative Transportation—Public Transportation Access
SS Credit 3.2	Alternative Transportation—Bicycle Storage and Changing Rooms
SS Credit 3.3	Alternative Transportation—Parking Availability

KEY TERMS

Adapted (or introduced) plants	These plants reliably grow well in a given habitat with minimal winter protection, pest control, fertilization, or irrigation once their root systems are established. Adapted plants are considered low maintenance and not invasive.
Albedo	See solar reflectance.
Alternative fuel vehicles	Vehicles that use low-polluting, nongasoline fuels such as electricity, hydrogen, propane, compressed natural gas, liquid natural gas, methanol, and ethanol. In LEED, efficient gas–electric hybrid vehicles are included in this group.
Aquifer	An underground water-bearing rock formation or group of formations that supply groundwater, wells, or springs.
Area-weighted SRI	A weighted average calculation that may be performed for buildings with multiple roof surfaces to demonstrate that the total roof area has an average solar reflectance index equal to or greater than that of a theoretical roof 75% of whose surfaces have an SRI of 78 and 25% have an SRI of 30.
Attendance boundary	Used by school districts to determine which students attend what school based on where they live.
Biodiversity	The variety of life in all forms, levels, and combinations, including ecosystem diversity, species diversity, and genetic diversity.
Brownfield	Real property whose use may be complicated by the presence or possible presence of a hazardous substance, pollutant, or contaminant.
Building density	The floor area of the building divided by the total area of the site (square feet per acre).
Building footprint	The area on a project site used by the building structure, defined by the perimeter of the building plan. Parking lots, landscapes, and other nonbuilding facilities are not included in the building footprint.

Campus or private bus	A bus or shuttle service that is privately operated and not available to the general public. In LEED, a campus or private bus line that operates within 1/4 mile of the project site and provides transportation service to the public can contribute to earning credits.
Carpool	An arrangement by which two or more people share a vehicle for transportation.
Comprehensive Environmental Response, Compensation and Liability Act, or CERCLA	CERCLA is more commonly known as Superfund. Enacted in 1980, CERCLA addresses abandoned or historical waste sites and contamination by taxing the chemical and petroleum industries and providing federal authority to respond to releases of hazardous substances.
Curfew hours	Locally determined times when lighting restrictions are imposed. When no local or regional restrictions are in place, 10:00 p.m. is regarded as a default curfew time.
Development footprint	The area affected by development or by project site activity. Hardscape, access roads, parking lots, nonbuilding facilities, and the building itself are all included in the development footprint.
Ecosystem	A basic unit of nature that includes a community of organisms and their nonliving environment linked by biological, chemical, and physical processes.
Emissivity	The ratio of the radiation emitted by a surface to the radiation emitted by a black body at the same temperature.
Endangered species	Threatened with extinction because of harmful human activities or environmental factors.
Erosion	A combination of processes or events by which materials of the earth's surface are loosened, dissolved, or worn away and transported by natural agents (such as water, wind, or gravity).
Eutrophication	The increase in chemical nutrients, such as the nitrogen and phosphorus often found in fertilizers, in an ecosystem. The added nutrients stimulate excessive plant growth, promoting algal blooms or weeds. The enhanced plant growth reduces oxygen in the land and water, reducing water quality and fish and other animal populations.
Footcandle (fc)	A measure of light falling on a given surface. One footcandle is defined as the quantity of light falling on a 1 square-foot area from a 1 candela light source at a distance of 1 foot (which equals 1 lumen per square foot). Footcandles can be measured both horizontally and vertically by a footcandle meter or light meter.
Fuel-efficient vehicles	Vehicles that have achieved a minimum green score of 40 according to the annual vehicle rating guide of the American Council for an Energy Efficient Economy.
Full cut-off luminaire	A luminaire that has zero candela intensity at an angle of 90 degrees above the vertical axis (nadir or straight down) and at all angles greater than 90 degrees from straight down. Additionally, the candela per 1,000 lamp lumens does not numerically exceed 100 (10%) at an angle of 80 degrees above nadir. This applies to all lateral angles around the luminaire.

Full-time equivalent (FTE)	Represents a regular building occupant who spends 40 hours per week in the project building. Part-time or overtime occupants have FTE values based on their hours per week divided by 40. Multiple shifts are included or excluded depending on the intent and requirements of the credit.
Greenfields	Sites not previously developed or graded that could support open space, habitat, or agriculture.
Greenhouse gases (GHGs)	These absorb and emit radiation at specific wavelengths within the spectrum of thermal infrared radiation emitted by the earth's surface, clouds, and the atmosphere itself. Increased concentrations of greenhouse gases are a root cause of global climate change.
Hardscape	The inanimate elements of the building landscaping. Examples include pavement, roadways, stone walls, concrete paths and sidewalks, and concrete, brick, and tile patios.
Heat island effect	The absorption of heat by hardscapes, such as dark, nonreflective pavement and buildings, and its radiation to surrounding areas. Particularly in urban areas, other sources may include vehicle exhaust, air conditioners, and street equipment; reduced airflow from tall buildings and narrow streets exacerbates the effect.
Horizontal footcandles	Horizontal footcandles occur on a horizontal surface. They can be added together arithmetically when more than one source provides light to the same surface.
Hybrid vehicles	Vehicles that use a gasoline engine to drive an electric generator and use the electric generator and/or storage batteries to power electric motors that drive the vehicle's wheels.
Hydrology	The study of water occurrence, distribution, movement, and balances in an ecosystem.
Impervious surfaces	Surfaces with a perviousness of less than 50% and promote runoff of water instead of infiltration into the subsurface. Examples include parking lots, roads, sidewalks, and plazas.
In situ remediation	Treatment of contaminants using technologies such as injection wells or reactive trenches. These methods employ the natural hydraulic gradient of groundwater and usually require only minimal disturbance of the site.
Infrared (or thermal) emittance	A parameter between 0 and 1 (or 0% and 100%) that indicates the ability of a material to shed infrared radiation (heat). The wavelength range for this radiant energy is roughly 5 to 40 micrometers. Most building materials (including glass) are opaque in this part of the spectrum and have an emittance of roughly 0.9. Materials such as clean, bare metals are the most important exceptions to the 0.9 rule. Thus, clean, untarnished galvanized steel has low emittance, and aluminum roof coatings have intermediate emittance levels.

Invasive plants	Invasive plants are nonnative to the ecosystem and likely to cause harm once introduced. These species are characteristically adaptable and aggressive, have a high reproductive capacity, and tend to overrun the ecosystems they enter. Collectively, they are among the greatest threats to biodiversity and ecosystem stability.
Light pollution	Waste light from building sites that produces glare, is directed upward to the sky, or is directed off the site. Waste light does not increase nighttime safety, utility, or security and needlessly consumes energy.
Light trespass	Light that is obtrusive and unwanted because of quantitative, directional, or spectral attributes. Light trespass can cause annoyance, discomfort, distraction, or loss of visibility.
Local zoning requirements	Local government regulations imposed to promote orderly development of private lands and prevent land-use conflicts.
Low-emitting vehicles	Vehicles that are classified as zero-emission vehicles (ZEVs) by the California Air Resources Board.
Mass transit	Transportation designed to transport large groups of persons in a single vehicle, such as a bus or train.
Master plan	In LEED, the master plan is an overall design or development concept for the school and associated buildings and site. This concept considers future use, growth, and contraction and includes ways to manage the facility and sustainable features. The master plan is typically illustrated with narrative descriptions, building plans, and site drawings of phases and planned development.
Mixed use	Mixed-use projects involve a combination of residential and commercial or retail components.
National Pollutant Discharge Elimination System (NPDES)	A permit program that controls water pollution by regulating point sources that discharge pollutants into waters of the United States. Industrial, municipal, and other facilities must obtain permits if their discharges go directly to surface waters.
Native (or indigenous) plants	Plants that are adapted to a given area during a defined time period and are not invasive. In North America, the term often refers to plants growing in a region prior to the time of settlement by people of European descent.
Open spaces	Open space areas are typically defined by local zoning requirements. If local zoning requirements do not clearly define open space, it is defined for the purposes of LEED calculations as the property area minus the development footprint; it must be vegetated and pervious, with exceptions only as noted in the credit requirements section. Only ground areas are calculated as open space. For projects located in urban areas that earn a Development Density and Community Connectivity credit, open space also includes nonvehicular, pedestrian-oriented hardscape spaces.
Open-grid pavement	Pavement that is less than 50% impervious and accommodates vegetation in the open cells.

Perviousness	The percentage of the surface area of a paving system that is open and allows moisture to soak into the ground below.
Preferred parking	Parking that is available to particular users and includes designated spaces close to the building (aside from designated handicapped spots), designated covered spaces, discounted parking passes, and guaranteed passes in a lottery system.
Previously developed sites	Sites that already have buildings, roadways, and parking lots or were graded or otherwise altered by direct human activities.
Property area	The total area within the legal property boundaries of a site; it encompasses all areas of the site, including constructed and nonconstructed areas.
Public transportation	Bus, rail, or other transit services for the general public that operate on a regular, continual basis.
Remediation	The process of cleaning up a contaminated site by physical, chemical, or biological means. Remediation processes are typically applied to contaminated soil and groundwater.
Residential area	Land zoned primarily for housing at a density of 10 units per acre or greater. These areas may have single-family and multifamily housing and include building types such as townhomes, apartments, duplexes, condominiums, or mobile homes.
Resource Conservation and Recovery Act (RCRA)	An EPA-established act that addresses active and future facilities and was enacted in 1976 to give the EPA authority to control hazardous wastes from cradle to grave, including generation, transportation, treatment, storage, and disposal. Some nonhazardous wastes are also covered under RCRA.
Retention ponds	Ponds that capture stormwater runoff and clear it of pollutants before its release. Some retention pond designs use gravity only; others use mechanical equipment, such as pipes and pumps, to facilitate transport. Some ponds are dry except during storm events; others permanently store water.
Safety and comfort light levels	Light levels that are local code requirements and must be adequate to provide a safe path for egress without over lighting the area.
Sedimentation	The addition of soil particles to water bodies by natural and human-related activities. Sedimentation often decreases water quality and can accelerate the aging process of lakes, rivers, and streams.
Shielding	A nontechnical term that describes devices or techniques that are used as part of a luminaire or lamp to limit glare, light trespass, or sky glow.
Site area	See property area.
Site assessment	An evaluation of a site's aboveground and subsurface characteristics, including its structures, geology, and hydrology. Site assessments are typically used to determine whether contamination has occurred, as well as the extent and concentration of any release of pollutants. Information generated during a site assessment is used to make remedial action decisions.

Sky glow	Sky glow is caused by stray light from unshielded light sources and light reflecting off surfaces that then enters the atmosphere and illuminates and reflects off dust, debris, and water vapor. Sky glow can substantially limit observation of the night sky, compromise astronomical research, and harm nocturnal environments.
Solar reflectance, or albedo	A measure of the ability of a surface material to reflect sunlight—visible, infrared, and ultraviolet wavelengths—on a scale of 0 to 1. Black paint has a solar reflectance of 0; white paint (titanium dioxide) has a solar reflectance of 1.
Solar reflectance index (SRI)	A measure of a material's ability to reject solar heat, as shown by a small temperature rise. Standard black (reflectance 0.05, emittance 0.90) is 0 and standard white (reflectance 0.80, emittance 0.90) is 100. For example, a standard black surface has a temperature rise of 90 F (50 C) in full sun, and a standard white surface has a temperature rise of 14.6 F (8.1 C). Once the maximum temperature rise of a given material has been computed, the SRI can be calculated by interpolating between the values for white and black. Materials with the highest SRI values are the coolest choices for paving. Because of the way SRI is defined, particularly hot materials can even take slightly negative values, and particularly cool materials can even exceed 100. (Lawrence Berkeley National Laboratory Cool Roofing Materials Database)
Stormwater pollution prevention plan	This plan includes all measures planned to prevent stormwater contamination, control sedimentation and erosion during construction, and comply with the requirements of the Clean Water Act.
Stormwater runoff	Water from precipitation that flows over surfaces into sewer systems or receiving water bodies. All precipitation that leaves project site boundaries on the surface is considered stormwater runoff.
Total suspended solids (TSS)	Particles that are too small or light to be removed from stormwater via gravity settling. Suspended solid concentrations are typically removed via filtration.
Transient users	Occupants who do not use a facility on a consistent, regular, daily basis. Examples include students in higher education settings, customers in retail settings, and visitors in institutional settings.
Vertical footcandles	Footcandles that occur on a vertical surface. They can be added together arithmetically when more than one source provides light to the same surface.

KEY TERMS

NONE

RELATED CREDITS

Locating a LEED-certified base building may make it easier to obtain numerous other LEED credits because the base building owner has already taken steps to make the building environmentally friendly.

INTENT

To encourage tenants to select buildings that employ best practices systems and green strategies.

REQUIREMENTS

Select a LEED-certified building.

IMPLEMENTATION

Work with real estate and leasing agents to find space in a LEED-certified base building.

DOCUMENTATION & CALCULATIONS

Obtain a copy of the base building's LEED certification certificate and final scorecard.

NOTES

None

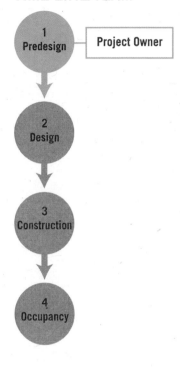

INTENT

To encourage tenants to select buildings that employ best practices systems and green strategies.

PATHS

Locate the tenant space in a building that has in place one or more of the following characteristics at the time of submittal. Each of the following options may also be met by satisfying the requirements of the corresponding LEED 2009 for New Construction credit.

Path 1: Brownfield Redevelopment

Path 2: Stormwater Design – Quantity Control

Path 3: Stormwater Design – Quality Control

Path 4: Heat Island Effect – Nonroof

Path 5: Heat Island Effect – Roof

Path 6: Light Pollution Reduction

Path 7: Water Efficient Landscaping – Reduce by 50%

Path 8: Water Efficient Landscaping – No Potable Water Use or No Irrigation

Path 9: Innovative Wastewater Technologies

Path 10: Water Use Reduction – 30% Reduction

Path 11: On-site Renewable Energy

Path 12: Other Quantifiable Environmental Performance

See the following pages (p. 28 - p. 49) for details
on the 12 Paths for SS Credit 1, Option 2.

KEY TERMS

BROWNFIELD

REMEDIATION

RELATED CREDITS

None

INTENT

To encourage tenants to select buildings that employ best practices systems and green strategies.

REQUIREMENTS

Option 1

Locate the tenant space in a building developed on a site documented as contaminated.

Option 2

Locate the tenant space in a building on a site classified as a brownfield by a local, state, or federal government agency.

In either case, effective remediation of contamination must have been completed.

IMPLEMENTATION

Select a base building that was constructed on a site formerly classified as a brownfield, catalogued by federal, state, or local authorities.

DOCUMENTATION & CALCULATIONS

Assemble information about the previous site contamination and remediation efforts undertaken.

NOTES

None

TIME LINE/TEAM

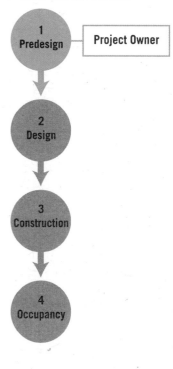

STANDARDS

U.S. EPA, Definition of Brownfields

ASTM E1903–97, Phase II Environmental Site Assessment, effective 2002

KEY TERMS

EROSION

IMPERVIOUS SURFACES

STORMWATER RUNOFF

RELATED CREDITS

SS Credit 1, Option 2, Path 3: Stormwater Design – Quality Control

SS Credit 1, Option 2, Path 4: Heat Island Effect – Nonroof

SS Credit 1, Option 2, Path 7: Water Efficient Landscaping – Reduce by 50%

SS Credit 1, Option 2, Path 8: Water Efficient Landscaping – No Potable Water Use or No Irrigation

SS Credit 1, Option 2, Path 10: Water Use Reduction – 30% Reduction

INTENT

To encourage tenants to select buildings that employ best practices systems and green strategies.

REQUIREMENTS

Option 1

Locate the tenant space in a building that prior to its development, had less than or equal to 50% imperviousness and has implemented a stormwater management plan that is equal to or less than the predevelopment 1½ year, 24-hour rate and quantity discharge.

Option 2

Locate the tenant space in a building that prior to its development had more than 50% imperviousness and has implemented a stormwater management plan that reduced the predevelopment 1½ year, 24-hour rate and quantity discharge by 25% of the annual on-site stormwater load. This mitigation can be achieved through a variety of measures, such as perviousness of site, stormwater retention ponds, and harvesting of rainwater for reuse.

IMPLEMENTATION

- Identify a space in a building that has implemented strategies to either maintain or reduce the amount of stormwater leaving the site as detailed in the credit requirements.

DOCUMENTATION & CALCULATIONS

- Determine the rates and quantities for pre- and post-development conditions for the required storm events.

- Determine the pervious and impervious areas, establishing a runoff coefficient for each.

Table 1 from the LEED Reference Guide for Green Interior Design and Construction, 2009. Page 14. Typical Runoff Coeffiicient.

Surface Type	Runoff Coefficient	Surface Type	Runoff Coefficient
Pavement, Asphalt	0.95	Turf, Flat (0 - 1% slope)	0.25
Pavement, Concrete	0.95	Turf, Average (1 - 3% slope)	0.35
Pavement, Brick	0.85	Turf, Hilly (3 - 10% slope)	0.40
Pavement, Gravel	0.75	Turf, Steep (> 10% slope)	0.45
Roofs, Conventional	0.95	Vegetation, Flat (0 - 1% slope)	0.10
Roof, Garden Roof (< 4 in)	0.50	Vegetation, Average (1 - 3% slope)	0.20
Roof, Garden Roof (4 - 8 in)	0.30	Vegetation, Hilly (3 - 10% slope)	0.25
Roof, Garden Roof (9 - 20 in)	0.20	Vegetation, Steep (> 10% slope)	0.30
Vegetation, Steep (> 10% slope)	0.10		

Equation 1 from the LEED Reference Guide for Green Interior Design and Construction, 2009. Page 14. Impervious Area (sf).

$$\text{Impervious Area (sf)} = \text{Surface Area (sf)} \times \text{Runoff Coefficient}$$

Equation 2 from the LEED Reference Guide for Green Interior Design and Construction, 2009. Page 15. Imperviousness (%).

$$\text{Imperviousness (\%)} = \frac{\text{Total Pervious Area (sf)}}{\text{Total Site Area (sf)}}$$

- List stormwater management strategies and record the percentage of rainfall that each is designed to handle.

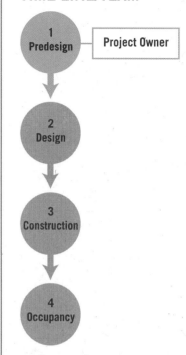

TIME LINE/TEAM

1 Predesign — Project Owner

2 Design

3 Construction

4 Occupancy

STANDARDS

None

NOTES

The 1½ year, 24-hour rate refer to a specific flow rate in cubic feet per second (cfs) that would be leaving the site. This would be a function primarily of the peak rainfall intensity (inches/hour) of the particular storm. The quantity refers to the volume of stormwater that leaves the site as a result of a 24-hour storm.

Stormwater values are based on actual local rainfall unless the actual exceeds the 10-year annual average local rainfall, in which case the 10-year annual average should be used.

KEY TERMS

IMPERVIOUS SURFACES

RETENTION PONDS

STORMWATER RUNOFF

TOTAL SUSPENDED SOLIDS (TSS)

RELATED CREDITS

SS Credit 1, Option 2, Path 2: Stormwater Design – Quantity Control

SS Credit 1, Option 2, Path 4: Heat Island Effect – Nonroof

SS Credit 1, Option 2, Path 7: Water Efficient Landscaping – Reduce by 50%

SS Credit 1, Option 2, Path 8: Water Efficient Landscaping – No Potable Water Use or No Irrigation

SS Credit 1, Option 2, Path 10: Water Use Reduction – 30% Reduction

INTENT

To encourage tenants to select buildings that employ best practices systems and green strategies.

REQUIREMENTS

Locate the tenant space in a building that has a stormwater treatment system designed to remove at least 80% of the average annual site area's total suspended solids (TSS) and 40% of the average annual site area's total phosphorus (TP).

IMPLEMENTATION

- Choose a base building that has a stormwater treatment system in place that meets the credit requirements.

- If the existing system does not meet the credit requirements, investigate opportunities to modify the site design. This might include constructing facilities to remove contaminants from the portion of stormwater that cannot be contained or reused on-site. Possible strategies include constructed wetlands, stormwater filtering systems, bioswales, retention basins, and vegetated filter strips.

DOCUMENTATION & CALCULATIONS

- In most cases, buildings that have implemented standard EPA or local best management practices will not need to complete any calculations. If designs far different from accepted best management practices have been developed and implemented, detailed engineering calculations may be required to demonstrate the reductions in TSS and TP.

- Develop a list of best management practices used to treat stormwater and a description of the contribution of each to stormwater filtration.

- For structural controls, list and describe the pollutant removal performance of each measure; determine the percentage of annual rainfall treated by each.

NOTES

None

TIME LINE/TEAM

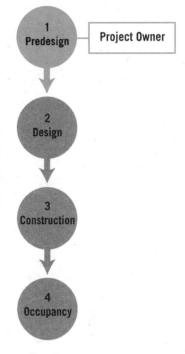

STANDARDS

U.S. EPA Management Measures for Sources of Non-Point Pollution in Coastal Waters

KEY TERMS

ALBEDO

EMISSIVITY

HEAT ISLAND EFFECT

IMPERVIOUS SURFACES

INFRARED (OR THERMAL) EMITTANCE

OPEN-GRID PAVEMENT

PERVIOUSNESS

SOLAR REFLECTANCE INDEX (SRI)

RELATED CREDITS

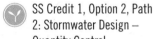 SS Credit 1, Option 2, Path 2: Stormwater Design – Quantity Control

SS Credit 1, Option 2, Path 3: Stormwater Design – Quality Control

SS Credit 1, Option 2, Path 7: Water Efficient Landscaping – Reduce by 50%

SS Credit 1, Option 2, Path 8: Water Efficient Landscaping – No Potable Water Use or No Irrigation

INTENT

To encourage tenants to select buildings that employ best practices systems and green strategies.

REQUIREMENTS

Option 1

Locate the tenant space in a building that provides shade (or will provide shade within five years of landscape installation); and/or uses light-colored or high-albedo materials with a solar reflectance index (SRI) of at least 29; and/or has open-grid pavement areas that individually or in total equal at least 30% of the site's nonroof impervious surfaces, such as parking areas, walkways, plazas, and fire lanes.

Option 2

Locate the tenant space in a building that has placed a minimum of 50% of parking spaces underground or covered by structured parking.

Option 3

Locate the tenant space in a building that has an open-grid pavement system (less than 50% impervious) for 50% of the parking lot area.

Exemplary Performance: This credit is eligible under SS Credit 1, Path 12: Other Quantifiable Environmental Performance.

IMPLEMENTATION

Choose a base building with physical characteristics that reduce its contribution to heat island effect.

DOCUMENTATION & CALCULATIONS

Option 1

Prepare a site plan that highlights all nonroof hardscape areas. Clearly label each portion of hardscape and add relevant information about surface compliance (i.e., the SRI values of reflective paving materials).

Option 2

Determine the total number of parking spaces and the portion covered. If applicable, assemble SRI values for the roofs that cover the parking areas.

Option 3

Prepare a site plan that highlights the areas covered by the open-grid pavement system for the parking lot area. Assemble information about the open-grid system used.

NOTES

The shaded area from landscaping can be the five-year projected area.

TIME LINE/TEAM

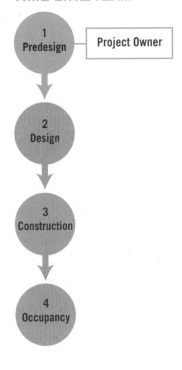

1 Predesign — Project Owner

2 Design

3 Construction

4 Occupancy

STANDARDS

None

KEY TERMS

ALBEDO

EMISSIVITY

INFRARED EMITTANCE

SOLAR REFLECTANCE INDEX (SRI)

RELATED CREDITS

 SS Credit 1, Option 2, Path 2: Stormwater Design – Quantity Control

SS Credit 1, Option 2, Path 3: Stormwater Design – Quality Control

SS Credit 1, Option 2, Path 7: Water Efficient Landscaping – Reduce by 50%

SS Credit 1, Option 2, Path 8: Water Efficient Landscaping – No Potable Water Use or No Irrigation

SS Credit 1, Option 2, Path 10: Water Use Reduction – 30% Reduction

INTENT

To encourage tenants to select buildings that employ best practices systems and green strategies.

REQUIREMENTS

Option 1

Locate the tenant space in a building whose roofing materials must meet the minimum requirements for at least 75% of the surface: low sloped—78 SRI; steep sloped—29 SRI.

Option 2

Locate the tenant space in a building that has installed a vegetated roof system on 50% or more of the roof.

Option 3

Locate the tenant space in a building that has a combination of high SRI roofs and vegetated roofs and that satisfies the area requirement in the calculation below.

Roof Type	Slope	SRI
Low-sloped roof	≤ 2:12	78
Steep-sloped roof	> 2:12	29

Exemplary Performance: This credit is eligible under SS Credit 1, Path 12: Other Quantifiable Environmental Performance.

IMPLEMENTATION

Choose a base building that has incorporated a highly reflective roof surface and/or a vegetated roof.

DOCUMENTATION & CALCULATIONS

All Options

● Complete calculations showing the percentage of roof area that is compliant. In order to complete the calculations, you will need the following information:

  ○ Total roof area in square feet excluding mechanical equipment, solar energy panels, and apertures (skylights, solar tubes, and the like);

  ○ Roof areas in square feet of qualifying reflective and vegetated roofing; and

  ○ Slope of roof.

● Information on roofing products, including their emittance percentages, reflectance percentages, SRI values, and slopes. Retain product specifications that verify product characteristics.

● Prepare roof drawings that show the total roof area and the areas of reflective materials or vegetated roof systems.

TIME LINE/TEAM

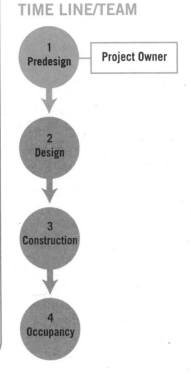

STANDARDS

ASTM International Standards

NOTES

None

KEY TERMS

LIGHT POLLUTION

LIGHT TRESPASS

SKY GLOW

RELATED CREDITS

EA Credit 1.1: Optimize
Energy Performance –
Lighting Power

EA Credit 1.2: Optimize
Energy Performance –
Lighting Controls

IEQ Credit 6.1: Controllability
of Systems – Lighting

INTENT

To encourage tenants to select buildings that employ best practices systems and green strategies.

REQUIREMENTS

Option 1

Locate the tenant space in a building whose nonemergency interior light fixtures are automatically controlled to turn off or have their input power reduced by at least 50% between 11:00 p.m. and 5:00 a.m.

Option 2

Locate the tenant space in a building whose exterior openings, such as windows, have shading devices that are automatically closed between 11:00 p.m. to 5:00 a.m.

IMPLEMENTATION

- Locate the project in a building with interior and exterior lighting equipment designed to eliminate light trespass from the building and the site, and include this requirement in the base building selection criteria.

DOCUMENTATION & CALCULATIONS

- Collect drawings showing the location of automatic controls and incorporate the sequence of operation for lighting into drawings and specifications or the building operation plan.

- If automatic shading devices are used, collect drawings of the shading devices, assemble specifications or product data showing that the shading devices result in transmittance of less than 10%, and incorporate the sequence of operation for automatic shading devices into drawings and specifications or the building operation plan.

NOTES

- Projects may have after-hours override as long as it lasts no more than 30 minutes.

- Projects operating 24 hours a day must use Option 2.

- Teams can also achieve this credit by meeting the requirements for LEED 2009 for New Construction SS Credit 8, Light Pollution Reduction.

TIME LINE/TEAM

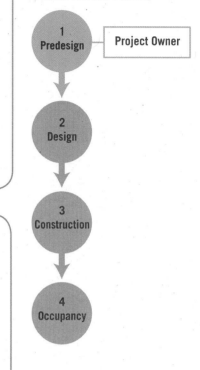

1 Predesign — Project Owner

2 Design

3 Construction

4 Occupancy

STANDARDS

None

| 2 Points | SS Credit 1: Site Selection, Option 2, Path 7: Water Efficient Landscaping – Reduce by 50% |

| 2 Additional Points | SS Credit 1: Site Selection, Option 2, Path 8: Water Efficient Landscaping – No Potable Water Use or No Irrigation |

KEY TERMS

ADAPTED (OR INTRODUCED) PLANTS

NATIVE (OR INDIGENOUS) PLANTS

RELATED CREDITS

SS Credit 1, Option 2, Path 2: Stormwater Design – Quantity Control

SS Credit 1, Option 2, Path 3: Stormwater Design – Quality Control

SS Credit 1, Option 2, Path 4: Heat Island Effect – Nonroof

SS Credit 1, Option 2, Path 5: Heat Island Effect – Roof

EA Credit 1: Optimize Energy Performance

INTENT

To encourage tenants to select buildings that employ best practices systems and green strategies.

REQUIREMENTS

SS Credit 1, Option 2, Path 7:

Locate the tenant space in a building that employs high-efficiency irrigation technology and/or uses water collected on-site to reduce potable water use for irrigation by 50%.

SS Credit 1, Option 2, Path 8:

Locate the tenant space in a building that uses only water collected on-site for all site irrigation OR does not have permanent irrigation systems.

IMPLEMENTATION

Choose a base building with water-efficient landscape irrigation that is designed to reduce or eliminate the use of potable water by incorporating features such as these:

- Landscaping with indigenous plants;
- Rainwater collection systems;
- High-efficiency irrigation strategies, such as microirrigation systems, moisture sensors, timers, and weather database controllers; and
- Graywater systems used for site irrigation.

NOTES

For projects pursuing SS Credit 1, Option 2, Path 8 via no irrigation, temporary irrigation systems can be used to help the landscape become established as long as they are removed within one year.

DOCUMENTATION & CALCULATIONS

Provide calculations showing the percentage reduction in water demand, and report what portion of irrigation will come from each nonpotable source (if any). In order to complete the calculations, you will need the following information:

- Landscape area of project in square feet;

- Square footage of each major vegetation type: trees, shrubs, ground-cover, mixed, and turfgrass;

- Characteristics of each vegetation type, including species factor (ks), density factor (kd), and microclimate factor (kme);

- Evapotranspiration rate (ETo) for the region; and

- Data on the irrigation system, including type and controller efficiency (CE).

Table 3 from the LEED Reference Guide for Green Interior Design and Construction, 2009. Page 40. Design Case (July).

Landscape Type	Area (sf)	Species Factor (k_s)	Density Factor (k_d)	Microclimate Factor (k_{mc})	K_L	ET_L	IE	TWA (gal)
Shrubs	1,200	Low 0.2	Avg 1.0	High 1.3	0.26	2.11	Drip	1,754.5
Mixed	3,900	Low 0.2	Avg 1.1	High 1.4	0.31	2.50	Drip	6,755
Turf grass	900	Avg 0.7	Avg 1.0	High 1.2	0.84	6.82	Sprinkler	6,122
Subtotal TWA (gal)								14,632
July rainwater and graywater harvest (gal)								(4,200)
TPWA (gal)								10,432

Table 4 from the LEED Reference Guide for Green Interior Design and Construction, 2009. Page 40. Baseline Case (July).

Landscape Type	Area (sf)	Species Factor (k_s)	Density Factor (k_d)	Microclimate Factor (k_{mc})	K_L	ET_L	IE	TWA (gal)
Shrubs	1,200	Avg 0.5	Avg 1.0	High 1.3	0.65	5.28	Sprinkler	6,316.4
Turf grass	4,800	Avg 0.7	Avg 1.0	High 1.2	0.84	6.82	Sprinkler	32,650.8
Subtotal TWA (gal)								38,967

Prepare a landscape plan showing a planting schedule and irrigation system.

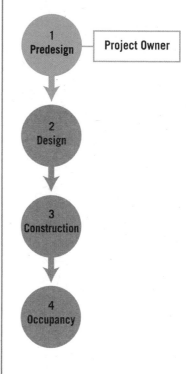

TIME LINE/TEAM

1 Predesign — Project Owner

2 Design

3 Construction

4 Occupancy

STANDARDS

None

KEY TERMS

BLACKWATER

COMPOSTING TOILET SYSTEM

GRAYWATER

NONPOTABLE WATER

ON-SITE WASTEWATER TREATMENT

POTABLE WATER

PROCESS WATER

TERTIARY TREATMENT

RELATED CREDITS

 SS Credit 1, Option 2, Path 10: Water Use Reduction – 30% Reduction

WE Prerequisite 1: Water Use Reduction

WE Credit 1: Water Use Reduction

INTENT

To encourage tenants to select buildings that employ best practices systems and green strategies.

REQUIREMENTS

Option 1

Locate the tenant space in a building that reduces potable water for building sewage conveyance by at least 50%.

Option 2

Locate the tenant space in a building that treats 100% of wastewater on-site or to tertiary standards.

IMPLEMENTATION

- Choose a base building that reduces potable water use by using low- or no-flush fixtures, including waterless urinals, composting toilets, or rain/graywater for toilet flushing.

- Choose a base building with an on-site wastewater treatment system such as an aerobic reactor or constructed wetlands.

NOTES

- The calculations require the use of a balanced, 1:1 gender ratio unless specific project conditions warrant an alternative.

DOCUMENTATION & CALCULATIONS

Option 1

- Using the calculations for WE Prerequisite 1: Water Use Reduction, determine the baseline and design case of only the flush fixtures (toilets and urinals), to determine whether potable water consumption is reduced by 50%.

Table 4 from the LEED Reference Guide for Green Interior Design and Construction, 2009. Page 49. Design Case.

Fixture Type	Daily Uses	Flowrate (gpf)	Occupants	Sewage Generation (gal)
Low-Flow Water Closet (Male)	0	1.1	150	0
Low-Flow Water Closet (Female)	3	1.1	150	495
Composting Toilet (Male)	1	0.0	150	0
Composting Toilet (Female)	0	0.0	150	0
Waterless Urinal (Male)	2	0.0	150	0
Waterless Urinal (Female)	0	0.0	150	0
Total Daily Volume (gal)				495
Annual Work Days				260
Annual Volume (gal)				128,700
Rainwater or Graywater Reuse Volume (gal)				(36,000)
Total Annual Volume (gal)				92,700

Table 5 from the LEED Reference Guide for Green Interior Design and Construction, 2009. Page 50. Baseline Case.

Fixture Type	Daily Uses	Flowrate (gpf)	Occupants	Sewage Generation (gal)
Water Closet (Male)	1	1.6	150	240
Water Closet (Female)	3	1.6	150	720
Urinal (Male)	2	1.0	150	300
Urinal (Female)	0	1.0	150	0
Total Daily Volume (gal)				1,260
Annual Work Days				260
Total Annual Volume (gal)				327,600

- Retain manufacturers' data showing the water consumption rates, manufacturer, and model of each fixture and fitting.

Option 2

- Determine the amount of wastewater compared with the capacity of the wastewater treatment system available.

- Compile information about the system schematics and capacity of any rainwater or graywater systems.

TIME LINE/TEAM

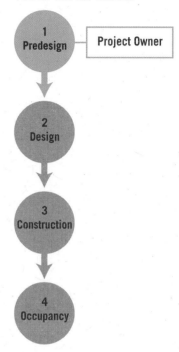

1 Predesign — Project Owner

2 Design

3 Construction

4 Occupancy

STANDARDS

The Energy Policy Act (EPAct) of 1992 (and as amended)

EPAct of 2005

2006 editions of the Uniform Plumbing Code or International Plumbing Code

1 Point

SS Credit 1: Site Selection, Option 2, Path 10: Water Use Reduction – 30% Reduction

KEY TERMS

BLACKWATER

NONPOTABLE WATER

NONWATER (OR COMPOSTING) TOILET SYSTEM

ON-SITE WASTEWATER TREATMENT

POTABLE WATER

PROCESS WATER

RELATED CREDITS

SS Credit 1, Option 2, Path 2: Stormwater Design – Quantity Control

SS Credit 1, Option 2, Path 3: Stormwater Design – Quality Control

SS Credit 1, Option 2, Paths 7 and 8: Water Efficient Landscaping

SS Credit 1, Option 2, Path 9: Innovative Wastewater Technologies

SS Credit 1, Option 2, Path 10: Water Use Reduction – 30% Reduction

WE Credit 1: Water Use Reduction

EA Prerequisite 1: Fundamental Commissioning of Building Energy Systems

EA Credit 2: Enhanced Commissioning

EA Credit 3: Measurement and Verification

INTENT

To encourage tenants to select buildings that employ best practices systems and green strategies.

REQUIREMENTS

Locate the tenant space in a building that reduces water use by at least 30% for the entire building and have an ongoing plan to require future occupants to comply.

Exemplary Performance: This credit is eligible under SS Credit 1, Path 12: Other Quantifiable Environmental Performance.

IMPLEMENTATION

Choose a base building that is equipped with water-conserving plumbing fixtures for the entire building.

DOCUMENTATION & CALCULATIONS

Complete the LEED Form Submittal Template showing the reduction of water use, listing plumbing fixtures by usage group. In order to complete the calculations, you will need the following information:

- Manufacturer, model number, and flush or flow rate for water closets, urinals, lavatory faucets, showers, kitchen sink faucets, and prerinse spray valves.

- Occupancy information, including the number of building occupants by occupancy type. It is also important to understand which FTE occupants use which restrooms if multiple locations with different fixtures are provided.

The percentage of water use is determined by dividing the design case by the baseline. The LEED Form Submittal Template will complete the final calculation.

NOTES

The calculations require the use of a balanced, 1:1 gender ratio unless specific project conditions warrant an alternative.

TIME LINE/TEAM

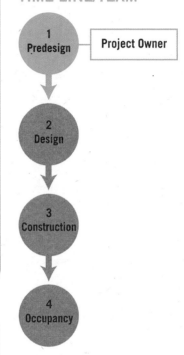

STANDARDS

The Energy Policy Act (EPAct) of 1992

EPAct of 2005

2006 editions of the Uniform Plumbing Code or International Plumbing Code

KEY TERMS

RENEWABLE ENERGY CERTIFICATES
(RECS)

INTENT

To encourage tenants to select buildings that employ best practices systems
and green strategies.

RELATED CREDITS

EA Prerequisite 1:
Fundamental Commissioning
of Building Energy Systems

EA Credit 3: Measurement
and Verification

REQUIREMENTS

Locate the tenant space in a building that supplies at least 2.5% (1 point)
or 5% (2 points) of the building's total energy use from on-site renewable
energy systems.

Exemplary Performance: This credit is eligible under SS Credit 1, Path 12:
Other Quantifiable Environmental Performance.

IMPLEMENTATION

Choose a base building that is equipped with an on-site renewable energy
system. **Eligible renewable energy systems include the following:**

- Photovoltaic systems;
- Wind energy systems;
- Solar thermal systems;
- Some biofuel-based electrical systems;
- Geothermal heating systems;
- Geothermal electric systems;
- Low-impact hydroelectric power systems; and
- Wave and tidal power systems.

Ineligible systems include the following:

- Architectural features;
- Passive solar strategies;
- Daylighting strategies; and
- Geo-exchange systems (ground-source heat pumps).

The sale of renewable energy certificates (RECs) is allowed from an on-site
renewable energy system that claims credit.

DOCUMENTATION & CALCULATIONS

- Determine the energy use for the project, demonstrate the portion of that supplied by on-site renewable energy systems, and identify a backup energy source.

- Prepare documentation from the project owner verifying the performance of the on-site renewable systems, confirming system capacity, and confirming that renewable energy is not double-counted.

NOTES

None

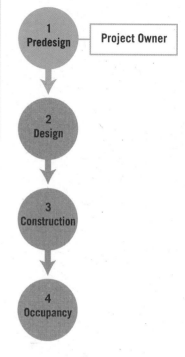

TIME LINE/TEAM

1 Predesign — Project Owner

2 Design

3 Construction

4 Occupancy

STANDARDS

ANSI/ASHRAE/IESNA 90.1–2007, Energy Standard for Buildings Except Low-Rise Residential

KEY TERMS

Refer to the key terms information under the selected credit.

RELATED CREDITS

Refer to the related credits information under the selected credit.

INTENT

To encourage tenants to select buildings that employ best practices systems and green strategies.

REQUIREMENTS

Locate the tenant space in a building that has other environmental benefits. An "other quantifiable environmental performance" characteristic is any green feature that was implemented according to the following:

● The requirements of another LEED rating system credit (not including the LEED for Commercial Interiors Rating System); or

● The exemplary performance criteria of any of the other paths (1 through 11) in this credit, where applicable.

IMPLEMENTATION

● Choose a base building that has achieved an environmental performance characteristic for at least one credit found in another LEED rating system.

● Achieve exemplary performance for eligible paths in SS Credit 1, Option 2, Paths 1 through 11.

● Submit a Credit Interpretation Request (CIR) to propose strategies not addressed by another LEED Rating System or within SS Credit 1, Option 2, Paths 1 through 11.

DOCUMENTATION & CALCULATIONS

Prepare a narrative, calculations, or other information that demonstrates the nature of the other environmental benefits delivered.

Refer to the documentation and calculation guidance section under the selected credit.

NOTES

None

TIME LINE/TEAM

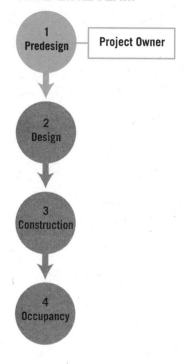

STANDARDS

Refer to the standards referenced for the credit from the other rating system used or under Paths 1 through 11.

KEY TERMS

BUILDING DENSITY

GREENFIELDS

MIXED-USE

RELATED CREDITS

 SS Credit 3.1: Alternative Transportation – Public Transportation Access

INTENT

To channel development to urban areas with existing infrastructure, protect greenfields, and preserve habitat and natural resources.

REQUIREMENTS

Option 1

Build on a previously developed site AND within an existing neighborhood with a density of 60,000 square feet per acre.

Option 2

Construct or renovate on a previously developed site AND within ½ mile of a residential area or a neighborhood with an average density of 10 units per acre AND within ½ mile of 10 basic services with pedestrian access between the building and the services.

IMPLEMENTATION

- Select sites within a developed neighborhood to curb urban sprawl by focusing development in areas with existing infrastructure, such as water lines, streets, and power. Additionally focus selection on sites that provide opportunities to walk, bike, or take public transportation.

- Select a building in a dense neighborhood.

NOTES

At least 8 of the 10 services must be existing, operational businesses. Anticipated services must demonstrate they will be operational within 12 months of the project opening.

The only basic service that can be counted more than once is restaurants: Two may be used.

Mixed-use projects may use only one service within the project boundary.

DOCUMENTATION & CALCULATIONS

For development density, keep records of the project site and building development area and prepare a project site vicinity plan that highlights the development density radius.

For community connectivity projects, create a site vicinity plan that highlights the ½-mile radius, the location and types of qualifying services, and the location of residential areas.

Table 1 from the LEED Reference Guide for Green Interior Design and Construction, 2009. Page 74. An illustration of a Sample Area Plan.

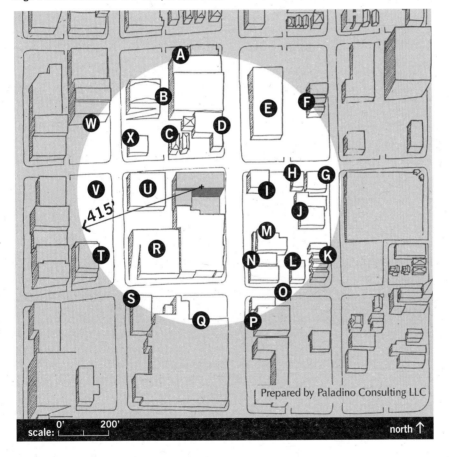

Prepared by Paladino Consulting LLC

scale: 0' 200'   north ↑

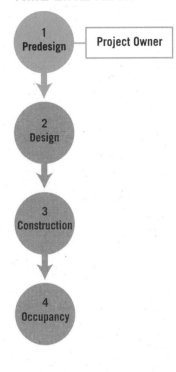

TIME LINE/TEAM

1 Predesign — Project Owner

2 Design

3 Construction

4 Occupancy

STANDARDS

None

KEY TERMS

MASS TRANSIT

RELATED CREDITS

 SS Credit 2: Development
Density and Community
Connectivity

INTENT

To reduce pollution and land development impacts from automobile use.

REQUIREMENTS

Provide dedicated pedestrian access to one of the options below.

Option 1: Rail Station Proximity

Locate the project in a building within ½ mile of a commuter rail, light rail,
or subway station.

Option 2: Bus Stop Proximity

Select sites that are within ¼ mile of two or more bus lines usable by
tenant occupants.

Exemplary Performance: Yes

IMPLEMENTATION

Select a site with public transportation access.

NOTES

If a light rail or subway station is sited, planned, and funded at the time
the project is completed, it satisfies the intent of this credit. If private
shuttle buses will be used to meet the requirements, they must connect
to public transportation and operate during the most frequent commuting
hours.

DOCUMENTATION & CALCULATIONS

- Identify local rail stations or bus routes serving the project building.

- Develop a site vicinity plan, to scale, and label walking paths between the project building's main entrance and rail stations or bus stops.

- On a site plan, draw a ¼- and a ½-mile radius from the main entrance. Identify the dedicated pedestrian routes and the bus and rail stops within these circles.

Figure 1 from the LEED Reference Guide for Green Interior Design and Construction, 2009. Page 82. Sample Area Drawing: Distance to Rail.

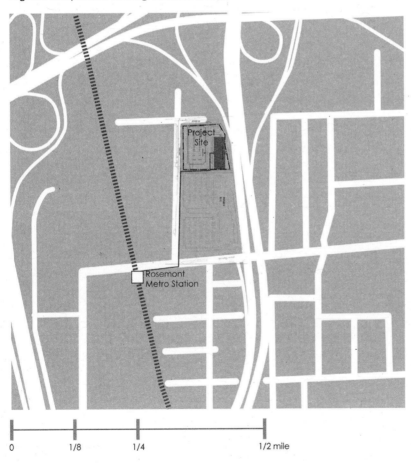

TIME LINE/TEAM

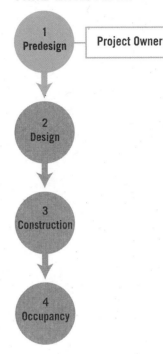

STANDARDS

None

KEY TERMS

FULL-TIME EQUIVALENT (FTE)

TRANSIENT USERS

RELATED CREDITS

None

INTENT

To reduce pollution and land development impacts from automobile use.

REQUIREMENTS

Provide secure bicycle racks and/or storage (within 200 yards of a main building entrance) for 5% or more of tenant occupants (measured at peak periods).

Provide shower and changing facilities in the building, or within 200 yards of a building entrance, for 0.5% of full-time equivalent (FTE) occupants.

Exemplary Performance: Yes

IMPLEMENTATION

- Choose a base building that has convenient access to safe bicycle pathways and secure bicycle storage areas for cyclists.

- Provide shower and changing areas easily accessible from bicycle storage areas.

DOCUMENTATION & CALCULATIONS

Provide a plan showing the location and quantity of bicycle storage and shower facilities and indicating the distance between the facilities and the building entry.

NOTES

Showers and changing rooms provided by health clubs must be free of charge, be available in sufficient quantities, and be provided under a minimum two-year contract between the tenant and the health club.

If changing rooms and showers are not within the tenant space, demonstrate that the required capacity will not be compromised by other users.

TIME LINE/TEAM

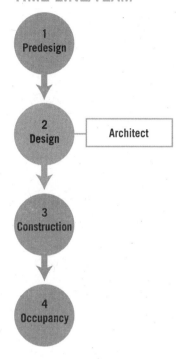

STANDARDS

None

KEY TERMS

CARPOOL

RELATED CREDITS

None

INTENT

To reduce pollution and land development impacts from automobile use.

REQUIREMENTS

Case 1: Projects With an Area Less Than 75% of the Total Building Area
Option 1
Parking spaces provided to tenants must not exceed the minimum number required by local zoning regulations, and preferred parking must be provided for carpools or vanpools capable of serving 5% or more of tenant occupants.
Option 2
No parking is provided or subsidized for tenant occupants.
Case 2: Projects With an Area 75% or More of the Total Building Area
Option 1
Parking capacity must not exceed minimum local zoning requirements, and preferred parking must be provided for carpools or vanpools capable of serving 5% of the building occupants.
Option 2
No new parking is added for rehabilitation projects, and preferred parking must be provided for carpools or vanpools capable of serving 5% of the building occupants.

Exemplary Performance: Yes

IMPLEMENTATION

- Provide preferred parking for carpool/vanpool vehicles.

- Do not provide any new parking, or do not exceed minimum local code.

- Confirm that the lease does not guarantee more spaces than the code requires.

DOCUMENTATION & CALCULATIONS

Develop a site plan showing parking spaces for tenants and the location and quantity of preferred spaces.

Assemble information about parking provided to the tenant space as well as zoning regulations and lease agreements, if applicable.

NOTES

None

TIME LINE/TEAM

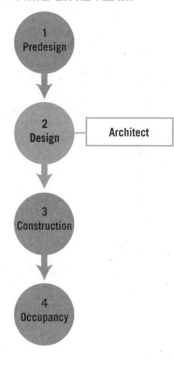

STANDARDS

None

1 What site factors are important to consider when selecting a building in which to locate a tenant space?

_____

_____

2 What types of neighborhoods are most likely to encourage building occupants to use alternative transportation modes?

_____

_____

3 What site attributes might have synergies with energy and water savings?

_____

_____

4 What are the benefits of locating a tenant space in a base building that has a **LEED** certification?

_____

_____

SS LEARNING ACTIVITIES

Sketch a simple diagram, highlighting the location of the bicycle parking, showers, and building to show compliance with the distance requirements.

PUT IT IN PRACTICE

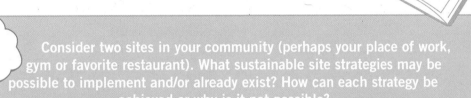

Consider two sites in your community (perhaps your place of work, gym or favorite restaurant). What sustainable site strategies may be possible to implement and/or already exist? How can each strategy be achieved or why is it not possible?

Strategies	Site A		Site B	
	Yes	No	Yes	No
Rainwater Harvesting				
Reduce Heat Island Effect				
On-Site Stormwater Management				
Minimize Landscape Water Usage				
Increase Access to Mass Transit				

THINK ABOUT IT

Consider a project with 20 FTE and 50 peak transient users. Determine the required amount of bicycle parking spaces and showers by completing the calculation below.

Occupants	Percentage Required	Number Required
20 FTE		
50 Peak Transient		
TOTAL		

TRY IT OUT

1 A project team is considering multiple base buildings for a new commercial interior. Proximity to which of the following will directly influence achievement of one or more credits within the Sustainable Sites category? (Select two.)

a) Proximity to mass transit such as buses

b) Proximity to local organic farms

c) Proximity to basic services such as parks

d) Proximity to dedicated bike boulevards

2 A LEED for Commercial Interiors project is locating in a building with 10,000 square feet of eligible roof area and is attempting to achieve SS Credit 1, Option 2, Path 5: Heat Island Effect – Roof. The roofing material has a solar reflectance index of 69. Twenty percent of the roof area has a low slope of 1:12, 60% of the roof area has a steep slope of 4:12, and the remaining 20% of the roof area is flat. The building owner is willing to install a vegetated roofing system for a portion of the flat roof area. How much of the flat roof area must be vegetated to qualify for this credit?

a) 0%; the project already qualifies

b) 25%

c) 50%

d) 75%

e) 100%

f) N/A; the project cannot achieve this credit as described above

3 Which are eligible systems that qualify under SS Credit 1, Option 2, Path 11: On-site Renewable Energy?

a) Biofuel systems powered by landfill gas

b) Biofuel systems powered by combustion of municipal solid waste

c) Biofuel systems powered by animal waste

d) Geo-exchange systems

e) Biofuel systems powered by unrestricted wood waste

4 A LEED for Commercial Interiors project is attempting to earn SS Credit 3.2: Alternative Transportation – Bicycle Storage and Changing Rooms. The peak occupancy is 100 people, and there are 10 FTE. How many secure facilities for bicycles and how many dedicated commuter showers and changing rooms must be provided to comply with the credit requirements?

a) 100 bicycle spaces, 5 showers

b) 25 bicycle spaces, 3 showers

c) 10 bicycle spaces, 1 shower

d) 5 bicycle spaces, 1 shower

5 A project team is locating in a building that is willing to modify the exterior lighting to address light pollution concerns. Which strategy below specifically addresses light trespass?

a) Installing dark sky compliant exterior fixtures

b) Installing highly efficient lamps and ballasts

c) Installing fixture shielding

d) Increasing the mounting height of fixtures

See Answer Key on page 200.

NOTES...

WATER EFFICIENCY

The importance of water to human life, plants, and wildlife can simply not be overestimated. It is critical to all forms of life, and, therefore, its proper management and discharge must be integral to any sustainable project. The impact of water use goes beyond how much water is consumed to the energy that it takes to get water to a site, followed by the treatment of the water after it leaves the site. The Water Efficiency (WE) category encourages the use of strategies and technologies that reduce the negative impacts associated with capturing, storing, delivering, and treating potable water that is consumed in buildings and their landscapes.

WHAT ABOUT WATER EFFICIENCY?

What technologies have allowed water savings in the past few decades? What emerging technologies and strategies hold promise to save even more water?

What uses require potable water? Are there any uses in typical buildings that may not require potable water?

Are there any no-cost water conservation strategies?

WATER EFFICIENCY

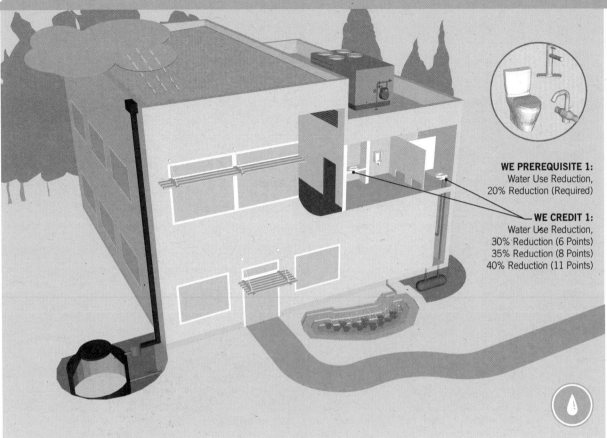

WE PREREQUISITE 1:
Water Use Reduction,
20% Reduction (Required)

WE CREDIT 1:
Water Use Reduction,
30% Reduction (6 Points)
35% Reduction (8 Points)
40% Reduction (11 Points)

THE OVERVIEW

Between increasing demand and shrinking supply, our water resources are strained, threatening both human health and the environment. In short, the current trend in the demand for water is completely unsustainable, with many cities projecting serious water shortages within ten years. The WE category addresses environmental concerns relating to building water use and disposal, and promotes the following measures:

- Reducing indoor potable water consumption;

- Saving energy through water conservation; and

- Practicing water-efficient landscaping.

WATER EFFICIENCY

SYNERGIES

Water efficiency is closely tied to the Energy and Atmosphere category. Heating water in buildings can account for 15% of a building's energy usage; using water efficiently within the building translates into energy savings. Savings are generated when the amount of heated water needed for a particular job can be reduced through smarter design or with simple technologies.

CATEGORY HIGHLIGHTS

- This category contains one prerequisite, which is to reduce the water use by 20% from the baseline.

- The WE credits require building a "baseline" case and then comparing it to the design case to determine the percentage savings beyond the baseline.

- The primary standard used to determine the baseline is the Energy Policy Act (EPAct) of 1992. It also contains some elements of subsequent rulings in the EPAct of 2005 and of the 2006 editions of the Uniform Plumbing Code and International Plumbing Code.

WATER EFFICIENCY CREDITS

CREDIT	TITLE
WE Prerequisite 1	Water Use Reduction
WE Credit 1	Water Use Reduction

KEY TERMS

Adapted (or introduced) plants	Plants that grow reliably well in a given habitat, with minimal winter protection, pest control, fertilization, or irrigation once their root systems are established. Adapted plants are considered low maintenance and not invasive.
Aquifer	An underground water-bearing rock formation or group of formations that supply groundwater, wells, or springs.
Automatic fixture sensors	Motion detectors that automatically turn on and turn off lavatories, sinks, water closets, and urinals. Sensors can be hard wired or battery operated.
Biochemical oxygen demand	A measure of how fast biological organisms use up oxygen in a body of water. It is used in water quality management and assessment, ecology, and environmental science.
Blackwater	Definitions vary, but wastewater from toilets and urinals is always considered blackwater. Wastewater from kitchen sinks (perhaps differentiated by the use of a garbage disposal), showers, or bathtubs is considered blackwater under some state or local codes.
Composting toilet system	See nonwater (or composting) toilet systems.
Conventional irrigation	The most common irrigation system used in the region where the building is located. A conventional irrigation system commonly uses pressure to deliver water and distributes it through sprinkler heads above the ground.
Drip irrigation	A system that delivers water at low pressure through buried mains and submains. From the submains, water is distributed to the soil through a network of perforated tubes or emitters. Drip irrigation is a high-efficiency type of microirrigation.
Evapotranspiration (ET) rate	The amount of water lost from a vegetated surface in units of water depth. It is expressed in millimeters per unit of time.
Graywater	Defined by the Uniform Plumbing Code (UPC) in its Appendix G, "Gray Water Systems for Single-Family Dwellings," as "untreated household waste water which has not come into contact with toilet waste. Graywater includes used water from bathtubs, showers, bathroom wash basins, and clothes washers and laundry tubs. It must not include waste water from kitchen sinks or dishwashers." The International Plumbing Code (IPC) defines graywater in its Appendix C, "Gray Water Recycling Systems," as "waste water discharged from lavatories, bathtubs, showers, clothes washers and laundry sinks." Some states and local authorities allow kitchen sink wastewater to be included in graywater. Other differences with the UPC and IPC definitions can likely be found in state and local codes. Project teams should comply with graywater definitions as established by the authority having jurisdiction in the project area.

Integrated pest management (IPM)	The coordinated use of knowledge about pests, the environment, and pest prevention and control methods to minimize pest infestation and damage by the most economical means while minimizing hazards to people, property, and the environment.
Landscape area	The total site area less the building footprint, paved surfaces, water bodies, and patios.
Metering controls	Controls that limit the flow time of water. They are generally manual-on and automatic-off devices, most commonly installed on lavatory faucets and showers.
Microirrigation	Microirrigation encompasses irrigation systems with small sprinklers and microjets or drippers designed to apply small volumes of water. The sprinklers and microjets are installed within a few centimeters of the ground; drippers are laid on or below grade.
Native (or indigenous) plants	Plants that are adapted to a given area during a defined time period and are not invasive. In North America, the term often refers to plants growing in a region prior to the time of settlement by people of European descent.
Nonpotable water	See potable water.
Nonwater (or composting) toilet systems	Dry plumbing fixtures and fittings that contain and treat human waste via microbiological processes.
On-site wastewater treatment	The transport, storage, treatment, and disposal of wastewater generated on the project site.
Potable water	Water that meets or exceeds the EPA's drinking water quality standards and is approved for human consumption by the state or local authorities having jurisdiction; it may be supplied from wells or municipal water systems.
Process water	Water used for industrial processes and building systems such as cooling towers, boilers, and chillers. It can also refer to water used in operational processes, such as dishwashing, clothes washing, and ice making.
Tertiary treatment	The highest form of wastewater treatment, it includes removal of organics, solids, and nutrients as well as biological or chemical polishing, generally to effluent limits of 10 mg/L biological oxygen demand (BOD) and 5 and 10 mg/L total suspended solids (TSS).
Xeriscaping	A landscaping method that makes routine irrigation unnecessary. It uses drought-adaptable and low-water plants as well as soil amendments such as compost and mulches to reduce evaporation.

Required | **WE Prerequisite 1: Water Use Reduction, 20% Reduction**

6 - 11 Points | **WE Credit 1: Water Use Reduction, 30%, 35%, or 40% Reduction**

KEY TERMS

AUTOMATIC FIXTURE SENSOR

BLACKWATER

NONPOTABLE WATER

NONWATER (OR COMPOSTING) TOILET SYSTEM

ON-SITE WASTEWATER TREATMENT

POTABLE WATER

PROCESS WATER

RELATED CREDITS

SS Credit 1, Option 2, Path 2: Stormwater Design – Quantity Control

SS Credit 1, Option 2, Path 3: Stormwater Design – Quality Control

SS Credit 1, Option 2, Paths 7 and 8: Water Efficient Landscaping

SS Credit 1, Option 2, Path 9: Innovative Wastewater Technologies

SS Credit 1, Option 2, Path 10: Water Use Reduction

EA Prerequisite 1: Fundamental Commissioning of Building Energy Systems

EA Credit 2: Enhanced Commissioning

EA Credit 3: Measurement and Verification

INTENT

To increase water efficiency within buildings to reduce the burden on municipal water supply and wastewater systems.

REQUIREMENTS

Reduce building potable water use by 20% (WE Prerequisite 1) and by 30%, 35%, or 40% (WE Credit 1) from the baseline.

Percentage Reduction	Points
20%	Required
30%	6
35%	8
40%	11

Exemplary Performance: Reduce building potable water use by 45%.

IMPLEMENTATION

Install low-flow and low-flush fixtures for toilets, urinals, restroom and kitchen faucets, showerheads, janitor sinks, metering faucets, and commercial prerinse valves.

DOCUMENTATION & CALCULATIONS

Provide calculations in the LEED Submittal Template showing the reduction of water use, listing plumbing fixtures by usage group. In order to complete the calculations, you will need the following information:

● Manufacturer, model number, and flush or flow rate for water closets, urinals, lavatory faucets, showers, kitchen sink faucets, and prerinse spray valves.

● Occupancy information, including the number of building occupants by occupancy type. It is important to understand which full-time equivalent (FTE) occupants use which restrooms if multiple locations with different fixtures are provided.

The percentage of water use is determined by dividing the design case by the baseline. Use the water use reduction calculator embedded within the LEED Submittal Template.

Retain manufacturers' data showing the water consumption rates, manufacturer, and model of each fixture and fitting.

NOTES

The calculations require the use of a balanced, 1:1 gender ratio unless specific project conditions warrant an alternative.

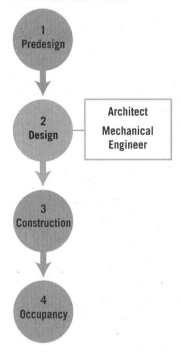

TIME LINE/TEAM

1 Predesign

2 Design — Architect / Mechanical Engineer

3 Construction

4 Occupancy

STANDARDS

The Energy Policy Act (EPAct) of 1992 (and as amended)

EPAct of 2005

The 2006 editions of the Uniform Plumbing Code or International Plumbing Code

1 What fixtures are covered by the water use reduction prerequisite and credit?

_____

_____

2 How can energy be saved by reducing water usage?

_____

_____

3 How are the Water Efficiency credits and Sustainable Sites credits related?

_____

_____

4 What is the baseline for the water use calculations?

_____

_____

Complete the water savings calculations for the WE prerequisite and credits for indoor water use reduction based on the information below.

- 100 FTE;
- Waterless urinals;
- Dual-flush water closets (0.8/1.6 gpf);
- Low-flow lavatories (0.5 gpm); and
- Conventional shower (2.5 gpm).

INVESTIGATE

Which of the following water efficiency systems do you use or have you seen?

ITEM	USED IT/SEEN IT?
Waterless urinals	
Dual-flush toilets	
Low-flow showerheads and faucets	
Drip irrigation systems	
Rainwater harvesting systems	

If you haven't seen one of the systems, see whether you can find one in your community.

THINK ABOUT IT

Identify the water utility that serves the building where you work and answer the following questions:

- What water conservation programs does your local water utility offer?
- What water use reduction strategies does the utility recommend?
- Does the utility incentivize water use reduction?
- How is water metered in the building where you work? Are there submeters?

WALK AROUND

1 When calculating the water use baseline for WE Prerequisite 1: Water Use Reduction, for a LEED for Commercial Interiors project, what flow rate should be used for public lavatories?

a) 0.5 gallons per minute

b) 2.5 gallons per minute

c) 2.2 gallons per minute

d) 1.0 gallons per minute

2 What are the environmental benefits of SS Credit 1, Option 2, Path 9: Innovative Wastewater Technologies? (Select three.)

a) Reduced potable water demand

b) Improved system redundancy

c) Increased local aquifer charge

d) Decreased need for chemical fertilizers

e) Lessened wastewater generation

3 Water contaminated with human waste is considered _____.

a) Brownwater

b) Graywater

c) Potable water

d) Blackwater

e) Discharge water

4 A project is attempting to reduce potable water use by 50% to earn SS Credit 1, Option 2, Path 7: Water Efficient Landscaping – Reduce by 50%. Which of the following can contribute to credit achievement? (Select two.)

a) Reduce landscaped area

b) Increase irrigation efficiency

c) Use groundwater sources

d) Design for a low landscape coefficient

5 A commercial office project is attempting WE Credit 1: Water Use Reduction, under LEED for Commercial Interiors. The project contains a break room within the tenant space that has a kitchen sink with a flow rate of 1.1 gallons per minute. The restrooms are included in the core and shell building and were not installed within the scope of the interior construction. What is the regulated water savings as applicable to WE Credit 1?

a) This project is not eligible for WE Credit 1.

b) 50%

c) 56%

d) Water savings cannot be determined without additional information.

See Answer Key on page 200.

ENERGY AND ATMOSPHERE

The Energy and Atmosphere (EA) category addresses the economic, social, and environmental consequences of energy use through conserving and generating energy in ways that minimize the negative impacts associated with most current energy systems. These impacts range from the depletion of fossil fuels, to contributions to global climate change, to the use of additional materials to develop new energy infrastructure as demand increases. EA specifically focuses on energy performance, building systems commissioning, responsible refrigerant use, performance verification, and the use of renewably generated energy.

WHAT ABOUT ENERGY AND ATMOSPHERE?

☀ Why do we try to conserve energy?

☀ What makes one source of energy better than another?

☀ Which building energy system(s) present the "lowest hanging fruit" in terms of reducing energy use?

☀ Why are some refrigerants better than others?

☀ How can energy performance be assured over time?

ENERGY AND ATMOSPHERE

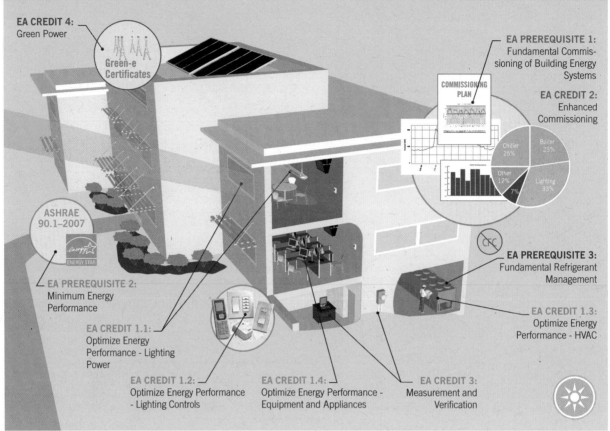

EA CREDIT 4: Green Power

Green-e Certificates

EA PREREQUISITE 1: Fundamental Commissioning of Building Energy Systems

COMMISSIONING PLAN

EA CREDIT 2: Enhanced Commissioning

Chiller 25%
Boiler 23%
Other 12%
7%
Lighting 33%

ASHRAE 90.1–2007

ENERGY STAR

CFC

EA PREREQUISITE 3: Fundamental Refrigerant Management

EA PREREQUISITE 2: Minimum Energy Performance

EA CREDIT 1.3: Optimize Energy Performance - HVAC

EA CREDIT 1.1: Optimize Energy Performance - Lighting Power

EA CREDIT 1.2: Optimize Energy Performance - Lighting Controls

EA CREDIT 1.4: Optimize Energy Performance - Equipment and Appliances

EA CREDIT 3: Measurement and Verification

THE OVERVIEW

Green interiors seek to address energy use in multiple ways. First and foremost, they reduce the amount of energy required to operate the tenant space. Additionally, energy use is tracked by monitoring devices and interpreted by building operators to catch deficiencies and identify opportunities for ongoing improvements. To further reduce environmental impacts from power generation, green interiors often purchase green power from their utility providers or on the open market.

In addition to energy use, the Energy and Atmosphere category addresses refrigerant use. Common refrigerants, which are typically used for air conditioning, are potent greenhouse gases that destroy Earth's stratospheric ozone.

This category focuses on four components of energy use within building interiors and their related atmospheric impacts:

ENERGY AND ATMOSPHERE

- Conserving energy (energy efficiency);
- Tracking building energy performance—design, commissioning, and monitoring;
- Managing refrigerants to minimize or eliminate atmospheric damage; and
- Using renewable energy.

SYNERGIES

Energy performance within a commercial interior is influenced by many aspects of the base building. In many cases, the building envelope and HVAC systems are designed and installed outside the scope of the interiors project. Where possible, collaboration between all team members and base building operators, beginning at project inception, is critical to optimal energy performance.

Many other aspects of the interior design and construction interact synergistically with energy performance. Consider, for instance, that the need for electric lighting is directly related to daylighting strategies and the reflectance of building finishes and furniture. The use of electric lights adds heat to the interior, thus creating the need for additional air conditioning in the summer months when energy demand peaks and is most expensive. Therefore, the reflectance of interior finishes can affect energy use for lighting, which in turn affects energy use for mechanical cooling equipment.

Water use also has a significant impact on energy use, as the heating and transporting of water for a variety of uses within the interior takes energy. Water-saving fixtures, such as low-flow lavatories, composting toilets, and waterless urinals, and water-efficient appliances, such as ENERGY STAR dishwashers and ice machines, reduce the energy costs associated with excessive water use.

Maintaining a high-quality indoor environment is often viewed as a trade-off with maximizing energy performance. However, although the use of active heating, cooling, and ventilation systems directly influences energy consumption, depending on the core and shell building chosen it is often possible to design an interior to reduce or eliminate the need for energy to maintain thermal comfort. Passive strategies, such as operable windows, stack effect ventilation, and the use of building mass to store and reject heat, can create meaningful energy savings while maintaining superior occupant comfort.

ENERGY AND ATMOSPHERE

CATEGORY HIGHLIGHTS

- This category represents 37 possible points out of a maximum 110 points available to LEED projects, more than any other category.

- A minimum level of energy performance is mandatory for all interiors projects seeking LEED 2009 for Commercial Interiors certification.

- Commissioning at a fundamental level is required of all LEED projects; enhanced commissioning goes beyond the mandatory levels and is worth additional points.

- Refrigerants containing CFCs must not be used in the HVAC&R systems.

- The purchase of renewable energy is recognized by LEED.

ENERGY AND ATMOSPHERE CREDITS

CREDIT	TITLE
EA Prerequisite 1	Fundamental Commissioning of Building Energy Systems
EA Prerequisite 2	Minimum Energy Performance
EA Prerequisite 3	Fundamental Refrigerant Management
EA Credit 1.1	Optimize Energy Performance—Lighting Power
EA Credit 1.2	Optimize Energy Performance—Lighting Controls
EA Credit 1.3	Optimize Energy Performance—HVAC
EA Credit 1.4	Optimize Energy Performance—Equipment and Appliances
EA Credit 2	Enhanced Commissioning
EA Credit 3	Measurement and Verification
EA Credit 4	Green Power

KEY TERMS

Baseline building performance	The annual energy cost for a building design intended for use as a baseline for rating above standard design, as defined in ANSI/ASHRAE/IESNA Standard 90.1–2007, Informative Appendix G.
Basis of design (BOD)	The basis of design includes design information necessary to accomplish the owner's project requirements, including system descriptions, indoor environmental quality criteria, design assumptions, and references to applicable codes, standards, regulations, and guidelines.
Chlorofluorocarbons (CFCs)	Hydrocarbons that are used as refrigerants and cause depletion of the stratospheric ozone layer.
Commissioning authority (CxA)	The individual designated to organize, lead, and review the completion of commissioning process activities. The CxA facilitates communication between the owner, designer, and contractor to ensure that complex systems are installed and function in accordance with the owner's project requirements.
Energy conservation measures	Installations or modifications of equipment or systems intended to reduce energy use and costs.
Energy simulation model or energy model	A computer-generated representation of the anticipated energy consumption of a building. It permits a comparison of energy performance, given proposed energy efficiency measures, with the baseline.
ENERGY STAR	A rating to measure a building's energy performance compared with that of similar buildings, as determined by the ENERGY STAR Portfolio Manager. A score of 50 represents average building performance.
Enhanced commissioning	A set of best practices that go beyond fundamental commissioning to ensure that building systems perform as intended by the owner. These practices include designating a commissioning authority prior to the construction documents phase, conducting commissioning design reviews, reviewing contractor submittals, developing a systems manual, verifying operator training, and performing a postoccupancy operations review.

Fundamental commissioning	A set of essential best practices used to ensure that building performance requirements have been identified early in the project's development and to verify that the designed systems have been installed in compliance with those requirements. These practices include designating a commissioning authority, documenting the owner's project requirements and basis of design, incorporating commissioning requirements into the construction documents, establishing a commissioning plan, verifying the installation and performance of specified building systems, and completing a summary commissioning report.
Halons	Substances used in fire-suppression systems and fire extinguishers, that deplete the stratospheric ozone layer.
Hydrochlorofluorocarbons (HCFCs)	Refrigerants that cause significantly less depletion of the stratospheric ozone layer than chlorofluorocarbons.
Hydrofluorocarbons (HFCs)	Refrigerants that do not deplete the stratospheric ozone layer, but may have high global warming potential. HFCs are not considered environmentally benign.
Leakage rate	The speed at which an appliance loses refrigerant, measured between refrigerant charges or over 12 months, whichever is shorter. The leakage rate is expressed in terms of the percentage of the appliance's full charge that would be lost over a 12-month period if the rate stabilized (EPA Clean Air Act, Title VI, Rule 608).
Lighting power density	The installed lighting power, per unit area.
Owner's project requirements	A written document that details the ideas, concepts, and criteria that are determined by the owner to be important to the success of the project.
Proposed building performance	The annual energy cost calculated for a proposed design, as defined in ANSI/ASHRAE/IESNA Standard 90.1–2007, Appendix G.
Refrigerants	The working fluids of refrigeration cycles that absorb heat from a reservoir at low temperatures and reject heat at higher temperatures.

Renewable energy certificates (RECs)	Tradable commodities representing proof that a unit of electricity was generated from a renewable energy resource. RECs are sold separately from electricity itself and thus allow the purchase of green power by a user of conventionally generated electricity.
Systems performance testing	The process of determining the ability of commissioned systems to perform in accordance with the owner's project requirements, the basis of design, and construction documents.

KEY TERMS

BASIS OF DESIGN (BOD)

COMMISSIONING AUTHORITY (CXA)

ENHANCED COMMISSIONING

FUNDAMENTAL COMMISSIONING

OWNER'S PROJECT REQUIREMENTS (OPR)

SYSTEMS PERFORMANCE TESTING

INTENT

EA Prerequisite 1:

To verify that the project's energy-related systems are installed and calibrated to perform according to the owner's project requirements, basis of design, and construction documents.

Benefits of commissioning include reduced energy use, lower operating costs, fewer contractor callbacks, better building documentation, improved occupant productivity, and verification that the systems perform in accordance with the owner's project requirements.

EA Credit 2:

To verify and ensure that the tenant space is designed, constructed and calibrated to operate as intended.

REQUIREMENTS

EA Prerequisite 1:

- Select a commissioning authority (CxA) to lead, review, and oversee the commissioning process.
    - The CxA must have documented experience commissioning at least two previous buildings.
    - For projects over 50,000 gross square feet, the CxA cannot be responsible for project design or construction.
    - The CxA must report directly to the project owner.
- Document the owner's project requirements (OPR) and the design team's basis of design (BOD).
- Include the commissioning requirements in the construction documents.
- Develop and implement a commissioning plan.
- Verify the installation and performance of the following systems:
    - HVAC&R systems (mechanical and passive) and associated controls;
    - Lighting and daylighting controls;
    - Domestic hot-water systems; and
    - Renewable energy systems (such as wind and solar).
- Complete a summary commissioning report.

REQUIREMENTS, CONTINUED

EA Credit 2:

- Select an independent, third-party CxA. In addition to the requirements of EA Prerequisite 1: Fundamental Commissioning, the CxA must meet the following criteria:
  - Not be an employee of the design firm; and
  - Not be an employee of, or contracted through, a construction company working on the project.
- The CxA must conduct one design review of the OPR, BOD, and design documents prior to development of the mid-construction documents and back-check his or her comments in the subsequent design submission.
- Review contractor submittals against the OPR and BOD.
- Develop a systems manual.
- Verify building operator training.
- Conduct a review of the building with operations and maintenance staff within 8 to 10 months of substantial completion, and create a plan for resolving outstanding commissioning-related issues.

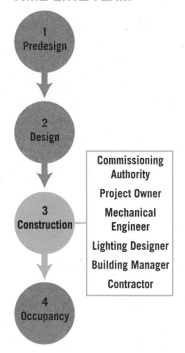

NOTES

For projects smaller than 50,000 gross square feet that are not pursuing EA Credit 2, Enhanced Commissioning, the CxA may be a qualified person on the design or construction team who has the required experience.

Continued on the next page

RELATED CREDITS

- SS Credit 1, Option 2, Path 6: Light Pollution Reduction
- SS Credit 1, Option 2, Path 11: On-site Renewable Energy
- WE Credit 1: Water Use Reduction
- EA Prerequisite 2: Minimum Energy Performance
- EA Prerequisite 3: Fundamental Refrigerant Management
- EA Credit 1.1: Optimize Energy Performance – Lighting Power
- EA Credit 1.2: Optimize Energy Performance – Lighting Controls
- EA Credit 1.3: Optimize Energy Performance – HVAC
- EA Credit 3: Measurement and Verification
- IEQ Prerequisite 1: Minimum Indoor Air Quality Performance
- IEQ Credit 1: Outdoor Air Delivery Monitoring
- IEQ Credit 2: Increased Ventilation
- IEQ Credit 5: Indoor Chemical and Pollutant Source Control
- IEQ Credit 6: Controllability of Systems
- IEQ Credit 7: Thermal Comfort

IMPLEMENTATION

EA Prerequisite 1:

- At the beginning of the design phase, select a commissioning authority with the proper experience and independence and complete the owner's project requirements. Instruct the design team to develop their respective basis of design documentation in accordance with these requirement.

- During design, incorporate the commissioning requirements in the project specification and develop a commissioning plan to govern the commissioning process.

- Once construction has been substantially completed, the CxA completes functional performance testing to ensure that the systems are operating as intended and meet the OPR.

- After functional testing has been completed, the CxA develops a summary commissioning report.

EA Credit 2:

- An independent CxA must be selected. An independent CxA is one who is not an employee of a company performing design or construction services for the project.

- During design, the CxA completes a commissioning design review prior to development of the mid-construction documents and back-checks his or her comments to ensure that issues have been addressed. Additionally, the CxA reviews the contractor's submittals as they are submitted to the design team for approval.

- After functional testing, a systems manual is developed. Additionally, the CxA verifies that building operator training has been given to the building's operations and maintenance staff.

- Once the building is operational, the CxA completes a walk-through 8 to 10 months after occupancy has been established.

DOCUMENTATION & CALCULATIONS

Numerous documents are created to guide, enforce, and facilitate reporting of the commissioning process. The mandatory documents for commissioning listed below should be retained by the design team and project owner.

EA Prerequisite 1:

- Commissioning plan;
- Commissioning requirements in construction documents;
- Commissioning report;
- Functional testing procedures;
- Owner's project requirements; and
- Basis of design.

EA Credit 2:

- Design review;
- Submittal reviews; and
- Systems manual.

While engineering calculations are generally necessary to develop functional testing procedures, no specific calculations are required for fundamental or enhanced commissioning.

STANDARDS

None

KEY TERMS

LIGHTING POWER DENSITY

ENERGY STAR

RELATED CREDITS

 EA Credit 1: Optimize Energy Performance

 EA Credit 4: Green Power

INTENT

To establish the minimum level of energy efficiency for the tenant space systems to reduce environmental and economic impacts associated with excessive energy use.

REQUIREMENTS

Design portions of the building covered by the tenant's scope of work to comply with the mandatory provisions of ASHRAE 90.1–2007, and achieve the prescriptive requirements or performance requirements of ASHRAE 90.1–2007.

Reduce lighting power density 10% below the referenced standard.

Install ENERGY STAR equipment for 50% (by rated power) of the eligible equipment installed within the tenant scope of work.

IMPLEMENTATION

Review the local building code and determine whether it is more or less stringent than ASHRAE 90.1–2007. If the local code is more stringent, design the commercial interior according to local code. If it is less stringent, ensure that the project complies with ASHRAE 90.1–2007.

Reduce lighting power as described in EA Credit 1.1: Optimize Energy Performance – Lighting Power.

Use ENERGY STAR equipment as described in EA Credit 1.4: Optimize Energy Performance – Equipment and Appliances.

The prerequisite requirements apply only to equipment that is installed within the scope of the tenant build-out. Base building systems that are not included within the commercial interiors project are excluded.

DOCUMENTATION & CALCULATIONS

The project team should retain copies of any code compliance documentation prepared by the designers.

For lighting power calculations, see EA Credit 1.1: Optimize Energy Performance – Lighting Power.

For ENERGY STAR calculations, see EA Credit 1.4: Optimize Energy Performance – Equipment and Appliances.

NOTES

This prerequisite does not apply to systems that are managed entirely by the landlord.

If the local code is more stringent than the applicable sections of ASHRAE 90.1–2007, it can be used in lieu of ASHRAE as long as documentation demonstrating that it is more stringent is provided.

California Title 24-2005, Part 6, is prequalified as equivalent to ASHRAE 90.–2007 for projects located in California; no additional confirmation is required.

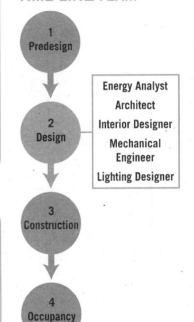

TIME LINE/TEAM

1 Predesign

2 Design

Energy Analyst
Architect
Interior Designer
Mechanical Engineer
Lighting Designer

3 Construction

4 Occupancy

STANDARDS

ANSI/ASHRAE/IESNA Standard 90.1–2007

ENERGY STAR®–Qualified Products

KEY TERMS

CHLOROFLUOROCARBONS (CFCS)

REFRIGERANTS

RELATED CREDITS

 EA Credit 1.3: Optimize Energy
Performance – HVAC

INTENT

To reduce stratospheric ozone depletion.

REQUIREMENTS

Do not use CFC-based refrigerants in tenant heating, ventilating, air-conditioning, and refrigeration (HVAC&R) systems installed within the LEED project scope of work.

IMPLEMENTATION

Specify and install only HVAC&R systems that use non-CFC refrigerants.

DOCUMENTATION & CALCULATIONS

Document the refrigerant type for all HVAC&R systems.

No calculations are associated with this prerequisite.

NOTES

HVAC&R systems can contain many types of refrigerants, such as chlorofluorocarbons (CFCs), hydrochlorofluorocarbons (HCFCs), and hydrofluorocarbons (HFCs), as well as natural refrigerants such as ammonia and carbon dioxide.

Base building HVAC&R units that are not installed within the scope of the commercial interiors project are not applicable to this prerequisite.

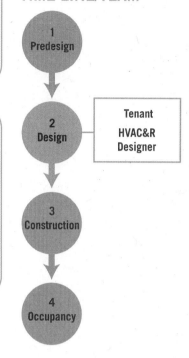

TIME LINE/TEAM

1 Predesign

2 Design — Tenant HVAC&R Designer

3 Construction

4 Occupancy

STANDARDS

None

KEY TERMS

LIGHTING POWER DENSITY

RELATED CREDITS

EA Prerequisite 1: Fundamental Commissioning

EA Prerequisite 2: Minimum Energy Performance

EA Credit 1.2: Optimize Energy Performance – Lighting Controls

EA Credit 2: Enhanced Commissioning

IEQ Credit 6.1: Controllability of Systems – Lighting

IEQ Credit 8.1: Daylight and Views – Daylight

INTENT

To achieve increasing levels of energy conservation beyond the referenced standard to reduce environmental and economic impacts associated with excessive energy use.

REQUIREMENTS

Reduce lighting power density at least 15% below the referenced standard; additional points are available for greater reductions.

Exemplary Performance: Yes

IMPLEMENTATION

Use only the lighting necessary to meet the program needs of the space, and use high-performance luminaires. Determine the lighting power allowance and connected lighting power for the space and calculate the lighting power reduction.

DOCUMENTATION & CALCULATIONS

Assemble ASHRAE lighting compliance documentation.

To calculate the lighting power reduction:

1. Determine the connected lighting power using the ASHRAE 90.1–2007 methodology.

2. Calculate the lighting power allowance.

3. Use the following formula to determine the lighting power reduction:

Equation 4 from the LEED Reference Guide for Green Interior Design and Construction, 2009. Page 157. Lighting Power Reduction.

$$\text{Lighting Power Reduction (watts)} = \text{Interior Lighting Power Allowance (watts)} - \text{Installed Interior Lighting Power (watts)}$$

Equation 4 from the LEED Reference Guide for Green Interior Design and Construction, 2009. Page 157. Lighting Power Density Percentage Reduction.

$$\text{Percentage Reduction (\%)} = \frac{\text{Lighting Power Reduction (watts)}}{\text{Interior Lighting Power Allowance (watts)}}$$

NOTES

Projects in California may use Title 24-2005, Part 6, in place of ASHRAE 90.1–2007.

The lighting power allowance can be calculated using either the Space-by-Space Method or the Whole Building Method as described in ASHRAE 90.1–2007.

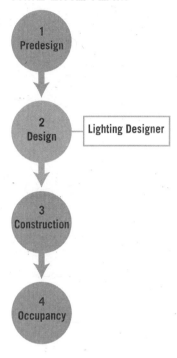

TIME LINE/TEAM

1 Predesign

2 Design — Lighting Designer

3 Construction

4 Occupancy

STANDARDS

ANSI/ASHRAE/IESNA Standard 90.1–2007

KEY TERMS

REGULARLY OCCUPIED SPACE

RELATED CREDITS

EA Prerequisite 1: Fundamental Commissioning

EA Prerequisite 2: Minimum Energy Performance

EA Credit 1.1: Optimize Energy Performance – Lighting Power

EA Credit 2: Enhanced Commissioning

IEQ Credit 6.1: Controllability of Systems – Lighting

IEQ Credit 8.1: Daylight and Views – Daylight

INTENT

To achieve increasing levels of energy conservation beyond the prerequisite standard to reduce environmental and economic impacts associated with excessive energy use.

REQUIREMENTS

Design the lighting control system to incorporate one or more of the following strategies:

- Daylight-responsive controls in all regularly occupied daylit spaces within 15 feet of windows or under skylights (one point);

- Daylight-responsive controls for at least 50% of the connected lighting load (one point); and

- Occupancy sensors for 75% of the connected lighting load (one point).

Exemplary Performance: Yes

IMPLEMENTATION

Develop an overall lighting control strategy, keeping in mind the interaction between different types of controls and how the system works as a whole. Consider how individual areas will be used and incorporate daylight as it is available.

DOCUMENTATION & CALCULATIONS

Lighting control plans, indicating the individual lighting control zones, should be developed by the lighting designer. When the interaction between various controls is complex, it is helpful to create a lighting control logic summary narrative so that the system functionality can be confirmed by the commissioning authority.

Calculations to determine how much of the lighting is controlled, in response to either daylight or occupancy sensors, should be completed according to the ASHRAE 90.1–2007 methodology similarly to EA Credit 1.1: Optimize Energy Performance – Lighting Power.

NOTES

Lighting can be controlled by occupancy sensors, daylight-responsive devices, or both.

Ideally, daylight-responsive lighting should be continuously dimmed; that is, adjusted in a continuous fashion based on the amount of daylight, although step dimming or simple on/off control is acceptable.

TIME LINE/TEAM

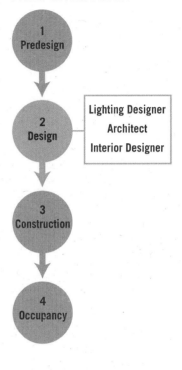

1 Predesign

2 Design

Lighting Designer
Architect
Interior Designer

3 Construction

4 Occupancy

STANDARDS

None

EA Credit 1.3: Optimize Energy Performance – HVAC

KEY TERMS

ENERGY SIMULATION MODEL

RELATED CREDITS

EA Prerequisite 1: Fundamental Commissioning

EA Prerequisite 2: Minimum Energy Performance

EA Prerequisite 3: Fundamental Refrigerant Management

EA Credit 1.1: Optimize Energy Performance – Lighting Power

EA Credit 1.2: Optimize Energy Performance – Lighting Controls

EA Credit 1.4: Optimize Energy Performance – Equipment and Appliances

EA Credit 2: Enhanced Commissioning

EA Credit 3: Measurement and Verification

IEQ Prerequisite 1: Minimum Indoor Air Quality Performance

IEQ Credit 1: Outdoor Air Delivery Monitoring

IEQ Credit 2: Increased Ventilation

IEQ Credit 5: Indoor Chemical and Pollutant Source Control

IEQ Credit 6.2: Controllability of Systems – Thermal Comfort

IEQ Credit 7: Thermal Comfort

INTENT

To achieve increasing levels of energy conservation beyond the prerequisite standard to reduce environmental and economic impacts associated with excessive energy use.

REQUIREMENTS

Option 1: Implement one or both of the following:

- Install HVAC systems that comply with the New Buildings Institute's Advanced Buildings™ Core Performance™ Guide, Sections 1.4 (Mechanical System Design), 2.9 (Mechanical Equipment Efficiency), and 3.10 (Variable Speed Control).

- Every solar exposure must have a separate control zone. Interior spaces must be separately zoned. Private offices and special occupancy areas (such as break rooms, kitchens, conference rooms, and so on) must have active ventilation controls capable of sensing space use and modulating the HVAC system in response to space demand.

Option 2: Reduce design energy cost by 15% for HVAC system components compared with ASHRAE 90.1–2007. Additional points are available for a 30% reduction.

Exemplary Performance: Yes, Option 2 only

IMPLEMENTATION

Option 1:

Design the HVAC system to comply with the relevant sections of the Advanced Buildings Core Performance Guide.

Design the HVAC system to recognize separate zones for each solar exposure and interior space.

Identify special occupancy areas and integrate demand control ventilation.

IMPLEMENTATION, CONTINUED

Option 2:

- Select a modeler.

- Determine the building segment.

- Select a modeling method.

- Obtain building information.

- Model the design case.

- Model the baseline case.

- Model an alternative baseline case if the core and shell building has more efficient elements than noted in ASHRAE 90.1–2007.

- Calculate the energy reduction.

DOCUMENTATION & CALCULATIONS

Retain HVAC control drawings that clearly identify the control logic, location of individual controls, and thermal control zones. If Option 2 is selected, list the baseline and design case equipment and summarize the energy cost by end use.

There are no calculations for Option 1. For Option 2, there are numerous subcalculations that are input into the energy model, such as lighting power density, fan sizing, and others, although the final computations are completed in the modeling software.

NOTES

None

TIME LINE/TEAM

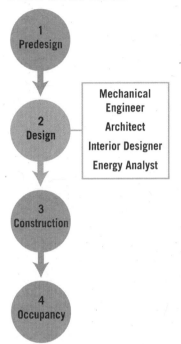

STANDARDS

ANSI/ASHRAE/IESNA Standard 90.1–2007

New Buildings Institute, Advanced Buildings™ Core Performance™ Guide

1 - 4 Points | **EA Credit 1.4: Optimize Energy Performance –
Equipment and Appliances**

KEY TERMS

ENERGY STAR

RELATED CREDITS

EA Prerequisite 2: Minimum
Energy Performance

INTENT

To achieve increasing levels of energy conservation beyond the prerequisite
standard to reduce environmental and economic impacts associated with
excessive energy use.

REQUIREMENTS

Install ENERGY STAR qualified equipment for at least 70% (by rated
power) of ENERGY STAR eligible equipment. Additional points are awarded
for higher levels of achievement.

Exemplary Performance: Yes

IMPLEMENTATION

Select equipment that meets ENERGY STAR criteria for energy performance.

DOCUMENTATION & CALCULATIONS

Request equipment cut sheets from the equipment vendor, indicating ENERGY STAR status.

To calculate the percentage of equipment for this credit:

- Identify all ENERGY STAR eligible equipment, and, of the eligible equipment, confirm which items are ENERGY STAR qualified.

- Identify the rated power for each piece of ENERGY STAR eligible equipment.

- Tally the combined rated power of both the ENERGY STAR eligible and ENERGY STAR qualified equipment.

- Finally, divide the combined ENERGY STAR–qualified rated power by the combined ENERGY STAR eligible rated power to determine the overall percentage of achievement.

NOTES

- ENERGY STAR eligible products are those that have a corresponding category under ENERGY STAR (regardless of the specific product's ENERGY STAR status).

- ENERGY STAR qualified products are ENERGY STAR eligible products that have attained ENERGY STAR due to superior energy performance.

- ENERGY STAR qualified products use 30% to 75% less electricity than other products.

TIME LINE/TEAM

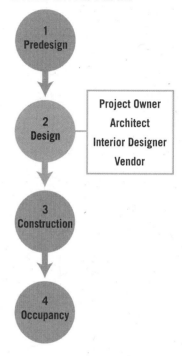

1 Predesign

2 Design

Project Owner
Architect
Interior Designer
Vendor

3 Construction

4 Occupancy

STANDARDS

ENERGY STAR®–Qualified Products

EA Credit 3:
Measurement and Verification

INTENT

To provide for the ongoing accountability and optimization of tenant energy and water consumption performance over time.

RELATED CREDITS

EA Prerequisite 1: Fundamental Commissioning

EA Prerequisite 2: Minimum Energy Performance

EA Credit 1: Optimize Energy Performance

EA Credit 2: Enhanced Commissioning

EA Credit 4: Green Power

REQUIREMENTS

Case 1. For Projects Less Than 75% of the Total Building Area:

Complete one or more of the following:

- Install submetering equipment.
- Negotiate a lease whereby energy costs are paid by the tenant and not included in the base rent.

Case 2. For Projects 75% or More of the Total Building Area:

- Install continuous metering equipment.
- Develop and implement a measurement and verification (M&V) plan.
- Provide a process for corrective action if energy savings are not being achieved.

IMPLEMENTATION

Case 1: Install submetering equipment to measure and record energy use within the tenant space.

Meter all energy sources, including electricity, natural gas, fuel oil, chilled water, and so on as applicable to the commercial interior.

Negotiate a lease whereby energy costs are paid by the tenant and not included in the base rent.

Case 2: Develop and implement a measurement and verification (M&V) plan, addressing the following:

- Accurate cataloging of baseline conditions;
- Verification of the complete installation and proper operation of new equipment and systems; and
- Confirmation of the quantity of energy and water savings, as well as energy and water cost savings that occur during the period of analysis.

DOCUMENTATION & CALCULATIONS

- For Case 2, develop an IPMVP-compliant measurement and verification plan.

- Where applicable, demonstrate that the tenant energy costs are paid by the tenant.

- Summarize the installed monitoring systems, demonstrating that the required end uses (Case 2) or energy sources (Case 1) are monitored and recorded.

- For Case 2, the calculation methodologies are detailed in IPMVP Volume 1.

NOTES

For Case 1, energy end uses may be measured on a single meter and reported together.

TIME LINE/TEAM

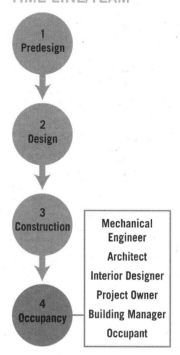

STANDARDS

International Performance Measurement and Verification Protocol (IPMVP) Volume I, Concepts and Options for Determining Energy and Water Savings, effective 2001, Efficiency Valuation Organization (EVO)

 **5 Points** | **EA Credit 4:**
Green Power

KEY TERMS

RENEWABLE ENERGY CERTIFICATES
(RECS)

RELATED CREDITS

 EA Credit 1: Optimize Energy
Performance

INTENT

To encourage the development and use of grid-source, renewable energy
technologies on a net zero pollution basis.

REQUIREMENTS

Purchase Green-e certified electricity for at least two years.

Exemplary Performance: Yes

IMPLEMENTATION

Select a Green-e certified power provider or purchase Green-e accredited
renewable energy certificates (RECs).

DOCUMENTATION & CALCULATIONS

Contract for green power or REC purchase.

NOTES

The quantity of green power purchased can be either 50% of the energy model prediction used for EA Credit 1.3: Optimize Energy Performance – HVAC, or can be the default rate of 8 kilowatt-hours per square foot per year.

TIME LINE/TEAM

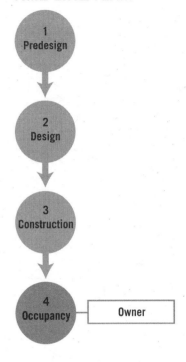

STANDARDS

Center for Resource Solutions, Green-e Product Certification Requirements

1 List some important strategies to reduce energy costs for commercial interiors projects.

_____

_____

2 What are the elements of commissioning?

_____

_____

3 What factors should be considered when selecting the HVAC&R system(s)?

_____

_____

4 Which energy end uses should be considered for EA Credit 3: Measurement and Verification?

_____

_____

Consider a core and shell building within your community and imagine that a new multistory interior is currently being designed for this base building. Evaluate options for energy cost reduction strategies given the building's specific characteristics. Consider lighting, equipment, HVAC&R, and other elements as appropriate. If you are participating as part of a study group, break into groups of three or four.

THINK ABOUT IT

Imagine you are the project owner for a new 10,000 square-foot commercial interiors project that is in the predesign phase within your community. The project is undecided as to whether it will pursue EA Credit 2: Enhanced Commissioning, although it will certainly pursue EA Prerequisite 1: Fundamental Commissioning of Building Energy Systems. Create a request for proposal (RFP) for a commissioning authority for the project. Be sure that the RFP identifies all the required aspects of fundamental commissioning, while requesting that the enhanced commissioning elements be provided as an add-on option. Ensure that the RFP identifies the qualifications necessary for the commissioning authority to successfully perform commissioning in accordance with LEED requirements.

PUT IT IN PRACTICE

Identify two commercial interiors in your community, preferably ones about whose operation you have specific knowledge. List some individual elements (lighting, HVAC, renewable energy systems, and so on). If you don't know some of their specific components, make a reasonable guess. Compare the components of the two interiors. Review which interiors have high-performance systems and which do not. Is there an opportunity for improvement in one or both?

INVESTIGATE

EA PRACTICE QUESTIONS

1 A project team is evaluating opportunities to downsize the mechanical system serving the tenant space. What strategy should be considered?

a) Install a high-performance chiller.

b) Decrease lighting power density.

c) Use non-CFC refrigerants.

d) Negotiate lower energy rates.

2 The Efficiency Valuation Organization (EVO) has established what standard to describe best practice techniques for measurement and verification of the tenant energy systems?

a) International Performance Measurement and Verification Protocol

b) Green-e Product Certification Requirements

c) The Montreal Protocol for Measurement and Verification

d) Standards and Measures for Performance Verification of Building Systems

e) Measurement and Performance Verification Practices

3 When documenting EA Credit 1.3: Optimize Energy Performance – HVAC, what information should be shown on the mechanical plans? (Select two.)

a) Location of automatic controls or sensors

b) Location of thermal zones

c) Location of ductwork

d) Thermal comfort calculations

e) Process for corrective action

4 A LEED for Commercial Interiors project is under construction, and the project team is attempting EA Credit 3: Measurement and Verification. The tenant space represents 40% of the total base building floor area. The base building has incorporated tenant submetering infrastructure to measure and record energy use within the tenant space. What else is required to achieve all available points under this credit?

a) Complying with Option A of the International Performance Measurement and Verification Protocol

b) Negotiating a lease under which energy costs are paid by the tenant

c) Confirming that the base building energy model will be recalibrated after one year of operation

d) Identifying a calculation methodology for calculating performance risk

A LEED for Commercial Interiors project has selected a base building and is entering early design. A commissioning authority has just been selected for the project and is contracted to complete EA Prerequisite 1: Fundamental Commissioning of Building Energy Systems, and EA Credit 2: Enhanced Commissioning. Once the owner's project requirements have been documented, what is the next step in the commissioning process?

a) Develop the functional testing procedures.

b) Complete the systems manual.

c) Document the basis of design.

d) Review the submittals.

e) Complete the design review.

See Answer Key on page 201.

NOTES...

MATERIALS AND RESOURCES

The Materials and Resources (MR) category focuses on reducing negative environmental impacts related to building materials and material waste generated during construction and operations. The MR category encourages selection of building materials that have reduced impacts associated with extraction, manufacturing, and transportation. The MR category also encourages recycling construction and building occupant waste to reduce the amount of waste that is disposed of in landfills and incinerators.

WHAT ABOUT MATERIALS AND RESOURCES?

What are the impacts of materials and resources used in the built environment?

Why should you recycle?

How do you know whether a building material is safe and healthy?

Where do interior building materials come from? What happens to building materials when their useful life is over?

Photo by Dale Photographic

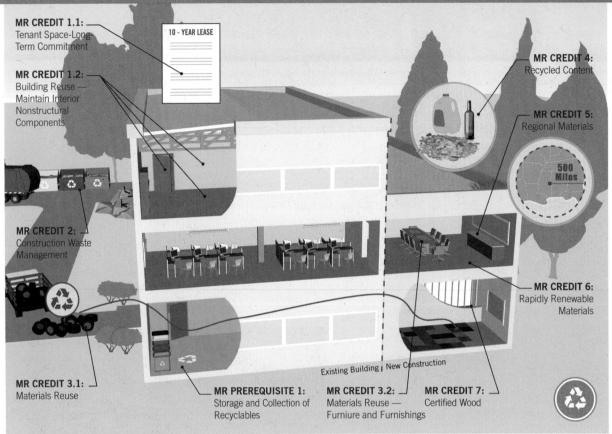

MR CREDIT 1.1:
Tenant Space-Long-Term Commitment

MR CREDIT 1.2:
Building Reuse — Maintain Interior Nonstructural Components

10 - YEAR LEASE

MR CREDIT 4:
Recycled Content

MR CREDIT 5:
Regional Materials

500 Miles

MR CREDIT 2:
Construction Waste Management

MR CREDIT 6:
Rapidly Renewable Materials

Existing Building | New Construction

MR CREDIT 3.1:
Materials Reuse

MR PREREQUISITE 1:
Storage and Collection of Recyclables

MR CREDIT 3.2:
Materials Reuse — Furniure and Furnishings

MR CREDIT 7:
Certified Wood

THE OVERVIEW

Demolition, construction, and subsequent operation of an interior fit-out generate enormous quantities of waste. The main issues to focus on are the environmental impact of materials used to construct the interior project and the minimization of landfill and incinerator disposal of materials taken out of the building. The MR category addresses the following measures:

- Selecting environmentally preferable materials;

- Reducing waste;

- Reducing the number of sources for materials and resources; and

- Reusing and recycling.

The Materials and Resources category promotes the selection of materials that have reduced environmental impacts compared with typical building materials. During construction, contractors can divert waste materials from landfills and/or incinerators to local recycling centers and significantly reduce the demand on local infrastructure. Recycling construction and demolition debris reduces demand for virgin resources and, in turn, reduces the environmental impacts associated with resource extraction, processing, and, in many cases, transportation.

Regardless of who specifies or provides them, all furniture and furnishings in the project should be included in calculations for LEED for Commercial Interiors. Because the value of these materials can be significant, the design and construction team should work closely with the facility manager, interior designer, furniture dealership, and installers from the outset.

Because of the variability of project scopes, the LEED for Commercial Interiors Rating System does not have an automatic default relationship between materials costs and the total construction cost.

SYNERGIES

The materials installed in a building may have an impact on the indoor environmental quality of the space depending on the types of finishes, adhesives, and sealants required. Careful materials specification also presents an opportunity to cut down on the amount of construction waste generated and the impact associated with bringing materials to the site.

CATEGORY HIGHLIGHTS

- Material cost must be consistent across all MR credits.

- Unlike in other LEED rating systems, project teams do not have the option to exclude certain materials such as furniture (exception: MR Credit 3.1: Materials Reuse).

- For MR credits, furniture and furnishings are defined as those materials included in Construction Specification Institute (CSI) MasterFormat™ Division 12. See Table 1 for the specific credits where they are included.

- Many opportunities for exemplary performance are achievable with careful planning and good specifications.

Table 1 from the LEED Reference Guide for Green Interior Design and Construction, 2009.
Page 209. Units of Measurement for Materials and Resources Credits

Material	MRc1.2 Building Reuse	MRc2 Construction Waste Management¹	MRc3.1 Material Reuse	MRc3.2 Material Reuse—Furniture	MRc4 Recycled Content	MRc5 Regional Materials	MRc5 Extracted and Manufactured Regionally	MRc6 Rapidly Renewable Materials	MRc7 Certified Wood
Mechanical	X		X	X	X²	X²	X²	X	
Electrical	X		X	X	X	X	X	X	
Ceiling	SF			X					
Floors	SF			X					
Walls	SF	Either Pounds or Cubic Feet but Consistent Throughout	Replacement Value ($)	X	Cost New ($) - Excludes Salvaged and Refurbished Materials counted in MRc3	Cost New ($)	Cost New ($)	Cost New ($)	Cost New ($) - Identify all wood-based materials, then exclude salvaged and refurbished material and postconsumer recycled wood fiber or portion of any products
Doors	SF			X					
Case Goods	SF			X					
Windows	SF			X					
All Other Construction Materials	X			X					
Furniture and Furnishings (CSI Division 12)	X	X	X	Replacement Value ($)					

¹ Do not include hazardous waste and excavated soil in MRc2 calculations.

MATERIALS AND RESOURCES CREDITS

CREDIT	TITLE
MR Prerequisite 1	Storage and Collection of Recyclables
MR Credit 1.1	Tenant Space—Long-Term Commitment
MR Credit 1.2	Building Reuse—Maintain Interior Nonstructural Components
MR Credit 2	Construction Waste Management
MR Credit 3.1	Materials Reuse
MR Credit 3.2	Materials Reuse—Furniture and Furnishings
MR Credit 4	Recycled Content
MR Credit 5	Regional Materials
MR Credit 6	Rapidly Renewable Materials
MR Credit 7	Certified Wood

KEY TERMS

Adaptive reuse	The renovation of a space for a purpose different from the original.
Alternative daily cover	Material (other than earthen material) that is placed on the surface of the active face of a municipal solid waste landfill at the end of each operating day to control vectors, fires, odors, blowing litter, and scavenging.
Assembly	An assembly is either a product formulated from multiple materials (for example, concrete) or a product made up of subcomponents (such as a workstation).
Assembly recycled content	The percentage of material in a product that is either postconsumer or preconsumer recycled content. It is determined by dividing the weight of the recycled content by the overall weight of the assembly.
Chain-of-custody (COC)	A tracking procedure for a product from the point of harvest or extraction to its end use, including all successive stages of processing, transformation, manufacturing, and distribution.
Chain-of-custody certification	An award for companies that produce, sell, promote, or trade forest products after audits verify proper accounting of material flows and proper use of the Forest Stewardship Council name and logo. The COC certificate number is listed on invoices for nonlabeled products to document that an entity has followed FSC guidelines for product accounting.
Construction and demolition debris	Waste and recyclables generated from construction and from the renovation, demolition, or deconstruction of preexisting structures. It does not include land-clearing debris, such as soil, vegetation, and rocks.
Construction waste management plan	A plan that at a minimum, identifies the diversion goals, relevant construction debris and materials to be diverted, implementation protocols, and parties responsible for implementing the plan.
Commingled	A mixture of several recyclables in one container.
Embodied energy	The energy used during the entire life cycle of a product, including its manufacture, transportation, and disposal, as well as the inherent energy captured within the product itself.
Existing area	The total area of the building structure, core, and envelope that existed when the project area was selected. Exterior windows and doors are not included.

Fly ash	The solid residue derived from incineration processes. Fly ash can be used as a substitute for Portland cement in concrete.
Forest Stewardship Council (FSC)	An independent, non-governmental, not-for-profit organization established to promote the responsible management of the world's forests. (http://www.fsc.org/about-fsc.html)
Interior nonstructural components reuse	Determined by dividing the area of retained components by the larger of (1) the area of the prior condition or (2) the area of the completed design.
Life-cycle assessment	An analysis of the environmental aspects and potential impacts associated with a product, process, or service.
Rapidly renewable materials	Agricultural products, both fiber and animal, that take 10 years or less to grow or raise and can be harvested in a sustainable fashion.
Refurbished materials	Products that could have been disposed of as solid waste. Once these products have completed their life cycles as consumer items, they are refurbished for reuse without substantial alteration of their forms. Refurbishing includes renovating, repairing, restoring, or generally improving the appearance, performance, quality, functionality, or value of a product.
Regionally extracted materials	Raw materials taken from within a 500-mile radius of the project site.
Regionally manufactured materials	Materials assembled as finished products within a 500-mile radius of the project site. Assembly does not include on-site assembly, erection, or installation of finished components.
Remanufactured materials	Items that are made into other products. One example is concrete that is crushed and used as a subbase.
Postconsumer recycled content	The percentage of material in a product that was consumer waste. The recycled material was generated by household, commercial, industrial, or institutional end users and can no longer be used for its intended purpose. It includes returns of materials from the distribution chain. Examples include construction and demolition debris, materials collected through recycling programs, discarded products (for example, furniture, cabinetry, and decking), and landscaping waste (such as leaves, grass clippings, and tree trimmings). (ISO 14021)

Preconsumer recycled content (formerly known as postindustrial content)	The percentage of material in a product that is recycled from manufacturing waste. Examples include planer shavings, sawdust, bagasse, walnut shells, culls, trimmed materials, overissue publications, and obsolete inventories. Excluded are rework, regrind, or scrap materials capable of being reclaimed within the same process that generated them. (ISO 14021)
Prior condition	The state of the project space at the time it was selected.
Prior condition area	The total area of finished ceilings, floors, and full-height walls that existed when the project area was selected. It does not include exterior windows and doors.
Retained components	Portions of the finished ceilings, finished floors, full-height walls and demountable partitions, interior doors, and built-in case goods that existed in the prior condition area and remain in the completed design.
Reused area	The total area of the building structure, core, and envelope that existed in the prior condition and remains in the completed design.
Soft costs	Expense items that are not considered direct construction costs. Examples include architectural, engineering, financing, and legal fees.
Source reduction	Source reduction reduces the amount of unnecessary material brought into a building. Examples include purchasing products with less packaging.
Sustainable forestry	The practice of managing forest resources to meet the long-term forest product needs of humans while maintaining the biodiversity of forested landscapes. The primary goal is to restore, enhance, and sustain a full range of forest values, including economic, social, and ecological considerations.
Tipping fees	Fees charged by a landfill for disposal of waste, typically quoted per ton.
Waste stream	The overall flow of waste from the building to a landfill, incinerator, or other disposal site.

Required | MR Prerequisite 1:
Storage and Collection of Recyclables

KEY TERMS

SOURCE REDUCTION

TIPPING FEES

WASTE STREAM

RELATED CREDITS

 ID Credit 1: Innovation in Design

INTENT

To facilitate the reduction of waste generated by building occupants that is hauled to and disposed of in landfills.

REQUIREMENTS

Allocate an area for the collection and storage of materials for recycling for the entire building. At a minimum, materials that are required to be recycled are paper, corrugated cardboard, glass, plastics, and metals.

IMPLEMENTATION

● Research local waste haulers and the services they provide.

● Distinguish existing locations within the base building that are dedicated to the collection and storage of recyclables.

● When the building's shared collection area is not sized to meet the needs of the entire building, the tenants must have their own dedicated and secure spaces.

DOCUMENTATION & CALCULATIONS

- Provide site and floor plans that highlight all recycling storage space.

- Acquire a letter from the landlord that outlines the building's recycling program.

- Calculations are not required for this prerequisite; however, guidance for the sizing of recycling areas is provided through recommended minimum areas based on the project's square footage.

- An additional source of guidance for the sizing of recycling areas is the California Integrated Waste Management Board's (CIWMB's) 2004 Statewide Waste Characterization Study, which gives quantity and composition estimates for commercial, residential, and self-hauled waste streams.

NOTES

- If a project does not occupy the entire building, it does not need to provide an outdoor collection area if a communal collection area exists or if the waste hauler or landlord arranges pickups within the tenant space.

- If projects locate in an already LEED-certified building, the team may need only to provide additional interior recycling, due to adequate storage and collection of recyclables that should already be present.

- If recycling collection and storage space is not available, another option is to conduct a waste stream audit of existing materials.

- Although there is no square footage requirement for the recycling area, relevant guidelines are provided in the LEED Reference Guide for Green Interior Design and Construction.

TIME LINE/TEAM

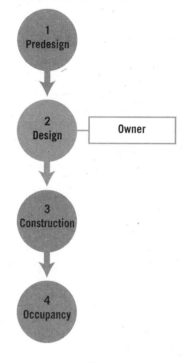

1 Predesign

2 Design — Owner

3 Construction

4 Occupancy

STANDARDS

None

1 Point

MR Credit 1.1:
Tenant Space – Long-Term Commitment

KEY TERMS

None

RELATED CREDITS

None

INTENT

To encourage choices that will conserve resources, reduce waste, and reduce the environmental impacts of tenancy as they relate to materials, manufacturing, and transport.

REQUIREMENTS

The tenant must commit to remain in the space for a minimum of 10 years.

IMPLEMENTATION

- Work with real estate and leasing agents to find space that will accommodate the project for a long period of time with anticipated growth and change.

- The requirement does not stipulate a relationship between the start of the lease period and the project construction activities.

DOCUMENTATION & CALCULATIONS

Retain a copy of the signed tenant lease agreement that specifies a minimum 10-year commitment.

NOTES

- Tenant lease agreements with an option to renew the lease after less than 10 years do not meet the requirements of this credit.
- Owning the space satisfies the credit requirement.

TIME LINE/TEAM

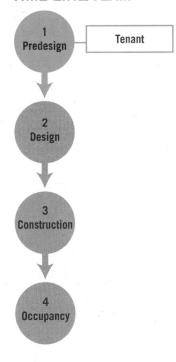

STANDARDS

None

KEY TERMS

ADAPTIVE REUSE

INTERIOR NONSTRUCTURAL
COMPONENTS REUSE

SOFT COSTS

RELATED CREDITS

MR Credit 2: Construction
Waste Management

MR Credit 3: Materials Reuse

INTENT

To extend the life cycle of existing building stock, conserve resources, retain cultural resources, reduce waste, and reduce environmental impacts of new buildings as they relate to materials manufacturing and transport.

REQUIREMENTS

The project must maintain at least 40% (one point) or 60% (two points) by area of the existing nonshell, nonstructural components. Interior nonstructural elements may include interior walls, doors, flooring, and ceiling systems.

Exemplary Performance: Yes

IMPLEMENTATION

- The interior designer or architect should develop a floor plan showing the location of finished ceilings and flooring, interior wall partitions, doors within the interior walls, exterior and party walls, and exterior windows and doors.

- Initially, it is important to confirm that the items that the team would like to reuse can actually be reused, then take the necessary steps to retain and maintain them in the finished work.

- Existing built-in case goods that will be reused should also be documented.

DOCUMENTATION & CALCULATIONS

- List the existing building elements, the corresponding element information, the total area of new and existing elements. Sum the total area of reused interior nonstructural elements.

Equation 1 from the LEED Reference Guide for Green Interior Design and Construction, 2009.
Page 225. Determination of Maintained Area.

$$\text{Interior Nonstructural Component Reuse (\%)} = \frac{\text{Total Retained Components Area (sf)}}{\text{Larger of Prior Condition OR Completed Design Area (sf)}} \times 100$$

- In order for fixed items, such as nonstructural walls and doors, to be included in this credit and count toward the percentage of reuse, they must perform the same function (for example, doors reused as doors).

- If materials are used for another purpose (such as doors made into tables), they can contribute toward the achievement of MR Credit 3.1, Materials Reuse, but they cannot count toward both credits.

NOTES

- Include full-height wall systems in MR Credit 1.2: Building Reuse – Maintain Interior Nonstructural Components.

- Projects that incorporate part of an existing building but do not meet the requirements for MR Credit 1.2 may apply the reused portion toward the achievement of MR Credit 2: Construction Waste Management.

- Division 12 items, including furniture and furnishings, are addressed in MR Credit 3.2: Materials Reuse – Furniture and Furnishings.

- Moving the demolition out of the project scope by making it the building owner's responsibility defeats the intent of this credit.

TIME LINE/TEAM

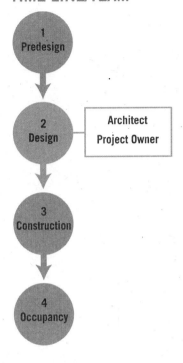

STANDARDS

None

1 - 2 Points | **MR Credit 2:**
Construction Waste Management

KEY TERMS

ALTERNATIVE DAILY COVER

CONSTRUCTION AND DEMOLITION DEBRIS

TIPPING FEES

RELATED CREDITS

 MR Credit 1.2: Building Reuse – Maintain Interior Nonstructural Components

 SS Credit 1, Option 2, Path 1: Brownfield Redevelopment

INTENT

To divert construction and demolition debris from disposal in landfills and incineration facilities. Redirect recyclable recovered resources back to the manufacturing process and reusable materials to appropriate sites.

REQUIREMENTS

Recycle and/or salvage at least 50% (one point) or 75% (two points) of the nonhazardous construction and demolition debris.

Develop and put into action a construction waste management plan.

Exemplary Performance: Yes

IMPLEMENTATION

- Develop and implement a construction waste management plan. The plan should identify construction haulers and recyclers to handle the various materials.

- Ensure that job-site personnel understand and participate in construction debris recycling, and maintain a current tally of diverted waste throughout construction.

- Request and hold onto the waste haul receipts, waste management reports, and/or spreadsheets to verify the recycling and/or salvage efforts throughout the length of the project.

- Salvaged materials may include furniture, computers and other electronic equipment, whiteboards, lockers, doors, lighting, and plumbing fixtures. Salvaged material can be diverted from landfills by donating them to charitable organizations such as Habitat for Humanity, reuse centers, other nonprofit organizations, or other buildings. In addition, materials sold to the community also count toward credit achievement.

- A project can separate construction waste on-site or have commingled construction waste sorted at a facility located off-site.

DOCUMENTATION & CALCULATIONS

● Track and keep a log of all construction waste generated by type, the quantities of each type that were diverted and landfilled, and the total percentage of waste diverted from landfill disposal.

● At a minimum, the construction waste management plan should identify diversion goals, construction debris and materials that will be diverted, implementation procedures, and who is responsible for implementing the plan.

● Calculations can be done by weight or volume but must be consistent throughout.

$$\text{Percentage of Waste Diverted (\%)} = \frac{\text{Total Quantity of Diverted Waste (Weight or Volume)}}{\text{Total Quantity of Waste (Weight or Volume)}} \times 100$$

NOTES

● A benefit of on-site separation is that it provides immediate feedback about the ongoing waste diversion efforts; however, it may require additional labor for implementation.

● Commingled recycling may increase recycling costs, but it may also simplify waste management efforts on-site and ensure that diversion rates will be high. This option is useful for projects that have tight space constraints and no room for collection bins.

TIME LINE/TEAM

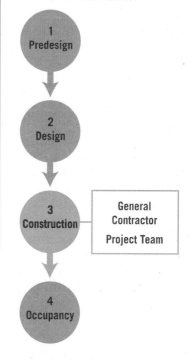

1 Predesign

2 Design

3 Construction — General Contractor / Project Team

4 Occupancy

STANDARDS

None

1 -2 Points | MR Credit 3.1:
Materials Reuse

KEY TERMS

REFURBISHED MATERIALS

REMANUFACTURED MATERIALS

RELATED CREDITS

MR Credit 1: Building Reuse

MR Credit 2: Construction Waste Management

MR Credit 3.2: Materials Reuse – Furniture and Furnishings

MR Credit 5: Regional Materials

INTENT

To reuse building materials and products to reduce demand for virgin materials and reduce waste, thereby lessening impacts associated with the extraction and processing of virgin resources.

REQUIREMENTS

Use salvaged, refurbished, or reused materials, the sum of which constitutes at least 5% (one point) or 10% (two points), based on cost, of building (construction) materials.

Exemplary Performance: Yes

IMPLEMENTATION

- Identify and reuse existing materials found both on- and off-site.

- Refurbished materials, such as a door that has been converted into a table, can count toward this credit or toward MR Credit 3.2: Materials Reuse, Furniture and Furnishings, but not both.

- Items that were "fixed" components on-site before construction began must no longer be able to serve their original functions and must then be installed for a different use or in a different location.

- Other reused materials found on-site that are retained and continue to serve their original function, such as door hardware, are eligible for this credit.

- Materials obtained off-site qualify as reused if they have been previously used. These materials may be purchased as salvaged, similar to any other project material, or they may be relocated from another facility, including ones previously used by the occupant.

DOCUMENTATION & CALCULATIONS

- Track costs according to CSI MasterFormat™ 2004 Edition Divisions 3–10, 31 (Section 31.60.00, Foundations) and 32 (Sections 32.10.00, Paving; 32.30.00, Site Improvements; and 32.90.00, Planting).

- Furniture and furnishings (CSI Division 12 components) are excluded from the calculations for this credit but are covered by MR Credit 3.2, Materials Reuse, Furniture and Furnishings.

- Mechanical, electrical, and plumbing components or appliances and equipment are not included in the calculations for this credit.

NOTES

- If walls, ceilings, and flooring continue to serve their original functions in the new project, they are excluded from this credit but are covered by MR Credit 1.2: Building Reuse – Maintain Interior Nonstructural Components.

- The salvaged materials from both on-site and off-site can also count towards MR Credit 5, Regional Materials, although they cannot be applied to any other MR credits.

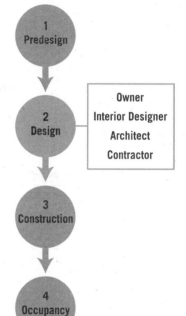

TIME LINE/TEAM

1 Predesign

2 Design

Owner
Interior Designer
Architect
Contractor

3 Construction

4 Occupancy

STANDARDS

None

1 Point | **MR Credit 3.2:**
Materials Reuse – Furniture and Furnishings

KEY TERMS

REFURBISHED MATERIALS

REMANUFACTURED MATERIALS

RELATED CREDITS

 MR Credit 2: Construction
Waste Management

 MR Credit 3.1: Materials Reuse

INTENT

To reuse building materials and products to reduce demand for virgin materials and reduce waste, thereby reducing impacts associated with the extraction and processing of virgin resources.

REQUIREMENTS

Use salvaged, refurbished, or used furniture and furnishings for 30% of the total furniture and furnishings budget.

Exemplary Performance: Yes

IMPLEMENTATION

- Identify opportunities to reuse furniture from the occupant's existing inventory.

- Consider obtaining used furniture from materials suppliers.

- Research and identify opportunities to reuse furniture, and consider salvaging and reusing systems furniture and furnishings, such as case pieces, seating, filing systems, decorative lighting, and accessories.

DOCUMENTATION & CALCULATIONS

- Track actual costs for salvaged, reused, or refurbished furniture and furnishings.

Equation 1 from the LEED Reference Guide for Green Interior Design and Construction, 2009. Page 241. Salvage Rate for Furniture and Furnishings.

$$\text{Salvage Rate (\%)} = \frac{\text{Replacement Value of Reused Furniture and Furnishings (sf)}}{\text{Total Value of New and Reused Furniture and Furnishings (sf)}} \times 100$$

NOTES

- For commercial interiors projects, furniture often is the largest single purchase. Furniture reuse is thus a strategy for considerable savings.

TIME LINE/TEAM

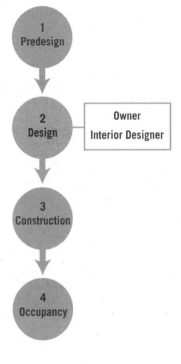

1 Predesign

2 Design — Owner / Interior Designer

3 Construction

4 Occupancy

STANDARDS

None

1 - 2 Points | MR Credit 4:
Recycled Content

KEY TERMS

ASSEMBLY RECYCLED CONTENT

FLY ASH

POSTCONSUMER RECYCLED CONTENT

PRECONSUMER RECYCLED CONTENT

RELATED CREDITS

MR Credit 2: Construction Waste Management

MR Credit 3: Materials Reuse

MR Credit 5: Regional Materials

MR Credit 6: Rapidly Renewable Materials

INTENT

To increase demand for building products that incorporate recycled content materials, thereby reducing impacts resulting from extraction and processing of virgin materials.

REQUIREMENTS

Use materials with recycled content such that the sum of postconsumer recycled content plus half of the preconsumer content constitute at least 10% (one point) or 20% (two points), based on cost, of the total value of the materials in the project.

Exemplary Performance: Yes

IMPLEMENTATION

- Establish goals for recycled content during the design phase and include them in the project specifications.

- Specify products and materials according to CSI MasterFormat 2004 classifications for Division 1 recycled-content requirements.

- Research which materials contain high levels of recycled content or verify which models of a certain product line feature the desired recycled-content values; examples are carpet and ceramic tile.

- Coordinate with subcontractors and suppliers to ensure that materials containing recycled content are available.

DOCUMENTATION & CALCULATIONS

- Record product names, manufacturers' names, costs, percentage postconsumer content, and percentage preconsumer content.

- Retain cut sheets to document the listed products' recycled content.

Equation 1 from the LEED Reference Guide for Green Interior Design and Construction, 2009.
Page 246. Recycled Content Value.

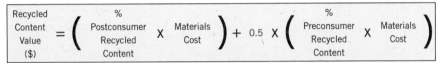

$$\text{Recycled Content Value (\$)} = \left(\text{\% Postconsumer Recycled Content} \times \text{Materials Cost} \right) + 0.5 \times \left(\text{\% Preconsumer Recycled Content} \times \text{Materials Cost} \right)$$

Equation 2 from the LEED Reference Guide for Green Interior Design and Construction, 2009.
Page 246. Percentage Recycled Content.

$$\text{Percentage Recycled Content} = \frac{\text{Total Recycled Content Value (\$)}}{\text{Total Materials Cost}} \times 100$$

- ○ Mechanical, electrical, and plumbing components cannot be included in this calculation.
- ○ Furniture and furnishings are included in the credit calculation.

NOTES

- Many standard materials contain recycled content because of how they are manufactured.

- Postconsumer recycled content has greater value because of its increased environmental benefit over the life cycle of the product.

- Reusing materials reclaimed from the same process in which they are generated—though good practice—does not contribute toward the recycled content of the material. In other words, putting waste back into the same manufacturing process from which it came is not considered recycling because it was not diverted from the waste stream. Reuse of materials includes rework, regrind, or scrap product (source: ISO 14021); examples are glass culls, which are often reused in the making of new glass, as well as planer shavings, plytrim, sawdust, chips, bagasse, sunflower seed hulls, walnut shells, other culls, trimmed materials, print overruns, overissue publications, and obsolete inventories.

TIME LINE/TEAM

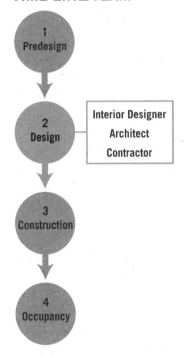

1 Predesign

2 Design — Interior Designer / Architect / Contractor

3 Construction

4 Occupancy

STANDARDS

International Standard ISO 14021–1999, Environmental Labels and Declarations, Self-Declared Environmental Claims (Type II Environmental Labeling)

1 -2 Points | # MR Credit 5:
Regional Materials

KEY TERMS

REGIONALLY EXTRACTED MATERIALS

REGIONALLY MANUFACTURED MATERIALS

RELATED CREDITS

 MR Credit 3: Materials Reuse

 MR Credit 4: Recycled Content

 MR Credit 6: Rapidly Renewable Materials

INTENT

To increase demand for building materials and products that are extracted and manufactured within the region, thereby supporting the regional economy and reducing the environmental impacts resulting from transportation.

REQUIREMENTS

Option 1 (one point)
Use a minimum of 20% of the combined value of construction and Division 12 (furniture and furnishings) materials and products that are manufactured regionally within a radius of 500 miles.

OR

Option 2 (two points)
Meet the requirements for Option 1.

Use a minimum of 10% of the combined value of construction and Division 12 (furniture and furnishings) materials and products extracted, harvested, or recovered, as well as manufactured, within 500 miles of the project.

Exemplary Performance: Yes

IMPLEMENTATION

- The point of manufacture is considered the place of final assembly of components into the building product that is furnished and installed by the trades workers.

- Evaluate this credit early in the design process because careful research may be required to determine what local products are available if products and construction components are assembled on-site. The individual components that are extracted within 500 miles of the site will be counted toward this credit.

- The general contractor should work with subcontractors and suppliers to verify availability of materials that are extracted, harvested, or recovered and manufactured locally.

- The contractor should run preliminary calculations based on the construction budget or schedule of values during the preconstruction phase. This will allow the construction team to focus on those materials with the greatest contribution to this credit as early as possible.

DOCUMENTATION & CALCULATIONS

- Create a list of purchased products that were manufactured, extracted, or harvested regionally.

- Record manufacturers' names, product costs, distances between the project and the manufacturer, and distances between the project and the extraction site.

- Retain cut sheets that document where the product was manufactured.

- In addition, for Option 2, prepare cut sheets to document extraction within a 500-mile radius of the project site.

Equation 1 from the LEED Reference Guide for Green Interior Design and Construction, 2009. Page 255. Percentage Local Materials.

$$\text{Percentage Local Materials} = \frac{\text{Total Cost of Local Materials (\$)}}{\text{Total Materials Cost (\$)}} \times 100$$

NOTES

- Using regional building materials reduces transportation activities and associated pollution.

- The support of regional manufacturers and labor forces retains capital in the community.

- If the material or product contains components that were sourced from a place within 500 miles but the final assembly was farther away, the product cannot be counted toward this credit.

TIME LINE/TEAM

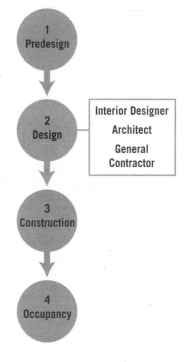

STANDARDS

None

1 Point | **MR Credit 6:**
Rapidly Renewable Materials

KEY TERMS

ASSEMBLY

EMBODIED ENERGY

LIFE-CYCLE ASSESSMENT

RAPIDLY RENEWABLE MATERIALS

RELATED CREDITS

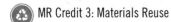 MR Credit 3: Materials Reuse

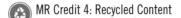 MR Credit 4: Recycled Content

 MR Credit 5: Regional
Materials

INTENT

To reduce the use and depletion of finite raw materials and long-cycle renewable materials by replacing them with rapidly renewable materials.

REQUIREMENTS

Use rapidly renewable construction and Division 12 (furniture and furnishings) materials and products for 5% of the total value of all materials and products used in the project, based on cost.

Exemplary Performance: Yes

IMPLEMENTATION

- Establish a goal for the use of rapidly renewable materials early in the design phase.

- Identify possible building materials that may be substituted with rapidly renewable products.

- Identify products and vendors in the project specifications and plans, and work with the general contractor to source acceptable alternatives.

DOCUMENTATION & CALCULATIONS

- Compile a list of rapidly renewable product purchases.

- Record manufacturers' names, materials costs, the percentage of each product that meets rapidly renewable criteria (by weight), and each compliant value.

- Retain cut sheets that document rapidly renewable criteria.

Equation 1 from the LEED Reference Guide for Green Interior Design and Construction, 2009.
Page 262. Percent Rapidly Renewable Materials.

$$\text{Percent of Rapidly Renewable Materials} = \frac{\text{Total Cost of Rapidly Renewable Material (\$)}}{\text{Total Materials Cost (\$)}} \times 100$$

NOTES

- Rapidly renewable building materials and products are made from plants that are replenished more quickly than traditional materials, as they are typically planted and harvested within a 10-year or shorter cycle.

- Sourcing rapidly renewable materials reduces the use of raw materials, whose extraction and processing have greater environmental impacts.

TIME LINE/TEAM

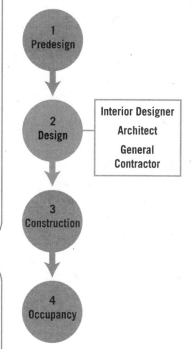

1 Predesign

2 Design — Interior Designer / Architect / General Contractor

3 Construction

4 Occupancy

STANDARDS

None

1 Point | **MR Credit 7:**
Certified Wood

KEY TERMS

CHAIN-OF-CUSTODY (COC)

CHAIN-OF-CUSTODY CERTIFICATION

SUSTAINABLE FORESTRY

RELATED CREDITS

 MR Credit 5: Regional Materials

IEQ Credit 4.4: Low-Emitting Materials – Composite Wood and Agrifiber Products

INTENT

To encourage environmentally responsible forest management.

REQUIREMENTS

A minimum of 50% of the new wood-based products and materials, including furniture, must be Forest Stewardship Council (FSC) certified.

Exemplary Performance: Yes, 95%

IMPLEMENTATION

- Specify in contract documents that wood products must come from forests that are certified as well managed according to the rules of the FSC, and require chain-of-custody (COC) documentation.

- Identify FSC-certified wood product suppliers. Research and specify quality grades that are most readily available from well-managed forests. Using lower grades of wood (for example, Architectural Woodwork Institute Grades 2 or 3 for lumber or veneer rather than Grade 1) can dramatically reduce pressure on forests, which produce only limited quantities of top-grade timber.

- Collect all vendor invoices for permanently installed wood products, FSC certified or not, purchased by the project contractor and subcontractors.

- Each vendor invoice must conform to the following requirements (except as noted below):
  - Each wood product must be identified on a line-item basis.
  - FSC products must be identified as such on a line-item basis.
  - The dollar value of each line item must be shown.
  - The vendor's COC certificate number must be shown on any invoice that includes FSC products.

DOCUMENTATION & CALCULATIONS

- Prepare the CSI MasterFormat™ 2004 Divisions 3–10 cost to determine the net construction materials cost.
- Prepare the CSI MasterFormat™ 2004 Division 12 (furniture and furnishings) cost to determine the net construction materials cost.

DOCUMENTATION & CALCULATIONS, CONTINUED

- Track certified wood purchases and retain associated COC documentation.
- Collect copies of vendor invoices for each certified wood product.
- Maintain a list that identifies the percentage of certified wood in each purchase.

Equation 1 from the LEED Reference Guide for Green Interior Design and Construction, 2009. Page 271. Certified Wood Material Percentage.

$$\text{Certified Wood Material Percentage} = \frac{\text{FSC-certified Wood Material Value (\$)}}{\text{Total New Wood Material Value (\$)}} \times 100$$

Equation 2 from the LEED Reference Guide for Green Interior Design and Construction, 2009. Page 272. Assembly FSC Certified Wood Material Value.

$$\text{Assembly FSC Certified Wood Material Value} = \frac{\text{Weight of FSC-certified Wood in Assembly}}{\text{Weight of Assembly}} \times \text{Assembly Value (\$)}$$

Equation 3 from the LEED Reference Guide for Green Interior Design and Construction, 2009. Page 272. Assembly New Wood Material Value.

$$\text{Assembly New Wood Material Value} = \frac{\text{Weight of New Wood in Assembly}}{\text{Weight of Assembly}} \times \text{Assembly Value (\$)}$$

TIME LINE/TEAM

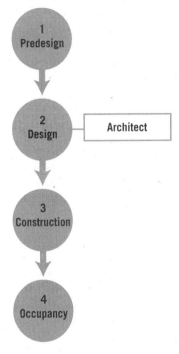

1 Predesign

2 Design — Architect

3 Construction

4 Occupancy

STANDARDS

Forest Stewardship Council's Principles and Criteria

NOTES

- Each wood products vendor that invoices FSC-certified products must be COC certified by an FSC accredited certifier.
- The negative environmental impacts of irresponsible forest practices can include forest destruction, wildlife habitat loss, soil erosion and stream sedimentation, water and air pollution, and waste generation.
- Exceptions: In some rare instances, it may not be practical for a vendor to invoice wood products on a line-item basis because the invoice would be dozens of pages long. In such cases, the invoice should indicate the aggregate value of wood products sold by the vendor. If the wood products are FSC certified, comply with the following requirements:
  - ○ The vendor's COC number must be shown on the invoice.
  - ○ The invoice must be supplemented by a letter from the vendor stating that the products invoiced are FSC certified.
  - ○ The invoice or the letter must state whether the products are FSC Pure, FSC Mixed Credit, or FSC Mixed (NN)%.

1 What are some benefits of implementing MR Credit 1.1: Tenant Space – Long-Term Commitment?

_____

_____

2 What are some referenced standards commonly used throughout the Materials and Resources category that provide testing, certification, and regulatory services? Briefly summarize what each standard does.

_____

_____

3 List the materials that should be addressed by a recycling program.

_____

_____

4 What are the environmental benefits of implementing an effective construction waste management plan?

_____

_____

5 What are some materials on the Construction Specification Institute (CSI) Master-Format Division 12 list?

_____

_____

MR LEARNING ACTIVITIES

1. Pick five materials and/or products used within your office or home and research whether they would comply with any of the Materials and Resources credits.
2. Locate designated recycling locations in your building and determine whether they meet LEED requirements.
3. Research local waste hauling companies to determine what construction waste materials can be recycled and how.

INVESTIGATE

Walk through an office or commercial or school building in your community to identify the materials listed below. Which Materials and Resources credit would each item contribute toward?

FEATURE	MR Credit 3	MR Credit 4	MR Credit 5	MR Credit 6	MR Credit 7
Workstation (salvaged from previous location)					
Wheatboard Kitchen Cabinetry					
Carpet					
Drywall					
Wooden Conference Table					
Steel Studs					
Ceramic Tiles					
Plywood					
Metal Shelving					
Other					

SITE VISIT

Identify a building product, currently existing or theoretical, that addresses as many of the concerns of the MR category as possible.

THINK ABOUT IT

1 A project team has specified doors that are made from 40% preconsumer recycled content and are manufactured at least 500 miles from the LEED project site from materials harvested and processed within 500 miles of the manufacturing location. The doors are certified as FSC Mixed (40)%. These doors represent 0.4% of the total building materials cost of permanently installed materials excluding mechanical, electrical, and plumbing components and specialty items such as elevators. Which LEED credits does this material qualify for?

   a) MR Credit 3:Materials Reuse, and MR Credit 4: Recycled Content

   b) MR Credit 3:Materials Reuse, and MR Credit 5: Regional Materials

   c) MR Credit 3: Materials Reuse, and MR Credit 7: Certified Wood

   d) MR Credit 4: Recycled Content, and MR Credit 5: Regional Materials

   e) MR Credit 4: Recycled Content, and MR Credit 7: Certified Wood

   f) MR Credit 5: Regional Materials, and MR Credit 7: Certified Wood

2 Reuse of which of the following existing elements contributes toward MR Credit 1.2: Building Reuse – Maintain Interior Nonstructural Components? (Select two.)

   a) Finished ceiling

   b) Exterior windows

   c) Carpet

   d) Wall framing

   e) Luminaires

3 A commercial interiors project has been constructed in a new core and shell building. The tenant build-out generated 10 tons of waste. Of the waste, 4 tons were recycled, 2 tons were soils that were donated to an adjacent site for infill purposes, 2 tons were incinerated to generate electricity, and the remaining 2 tons were sent to the landfill. What is the overall diversion rate as applicable to MR Credit 2: Construction Waste Management?

   a) 40%

   b) 50%

   c) 60%

   d) 70%

   e) 80%

4 In addition to paper, corrugated cardboard, glass, and plastics, which material must be provided an easily accessible area for collection to comply with MR Prerequisite 1: Storage and Collection of Recyclables?

   a) Food scraps

   b) Yard trimmings

   c) Wood

   d) Metals

   e) Rubber

5 Rapidly renewable materials are typically harvested within a _____?

   a) 2-year or shorter cycle

   b) 5-year or shorter cycle

   c) 10-year or shorter cycle

   d) 15-year or shorter cycle

See Answer Key on page 201.

The Indoor Environmental Quality (IEQ) category addresses the significant effects that the quality of the interior environment has on occupants. This category seeks to improve ventilation, manage air contaminants, and improve occupant comfort.

WHAT ABOUT INDOOR ENVIRONMENTAL QUALITY?

What are the various aspects that contribute toward indoor environmental quality?

What are the indoor environmental factors that affect human health?

What are the health risks associated with environmental tobacco smoke?

How do indoor environmental conditions affect your productivity, comfort, and mood?

Can you have too much ventilation?

Photo by Eric Laignel

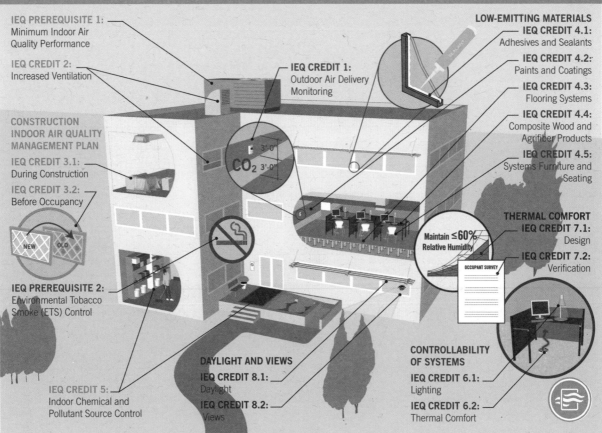

IEQ PREREQUISITE 1:
Minimum Indoor Air
Quality Performance

IEQ CREDIT 2:
Increased Ventilation

CONSTRUCTION
INDOOR AIR QUALITY
MANAGEMENT PLAN
IEQ CREDIT 3.1:
During Construction

IEQ CREDIT 3.2:
Before Occupancy

NEW   OLD

IEQ PREREQUISITE 2:
Environmental Tobacco
Smoke (ETS) Control

IEQ CREDIT 5:
Indoor Chemical and
Pollutant Source Control

IEQ CREDIT 1:
Outdoor Air Delivery
Monitoring

CO_2 3'-0"   3'-0"

DAYLIGHT AND VIEWS
IEQ CREDIT 8.1:
Daylight
IEQ CREDIT 8.2:
Views

LOW-EMITTING MATERIALS
IEQ CREDIT 4.1:
Adhesives and Sealants

IEQ CREDIT 4.2:
Paints and Coatings

IEQ CREDIT 4.3:
Flooring Systems

IEQ CREDIT 4.4:
Composite Wood and
Agrifiber Products

IEQ CREDIT 4.5:
Systems Furniture and
Seating

THERMAL COMFORT
IEQ CREDIT 7.1:
Design

IEQ CREDIT 7.2:
Verification

Maintain ≤60%
Relative Humidity

OCCUPANT SURVEY

CONTROLLABILITY
OF SYSTEMS
IEQ CREDIT 6.1:
Lighting
IEQ CREDIT 6.2:
Thermal Comfort

THE OVERVIEW

On average, Americans spend 90% of their time indoors, where pollutant levels may be two to five times higher, and occasionally more than 100 times higher, than outdoor levels. Over the past 20 years, research and experience have improved our understanding of what is involved in attaining high indoor environmental quality and revealed manufacturing and construction practices that can prevent many indoor environmental quality problems. This credit category addresses environmental concerns relating to indoor environmental quality; occupants' health, comfort, and productivity; ventilation; and air contaminant mitigation. The IEQ prerequisites and credits focus on the following strategies:

- Improving ventilation;

- Managing air contaminants;

- Specifying less toxic materials;

- Allowing occupants to have control over their environment; and

- Providing daylight and views.

INDOOR ENVIRONMENTAL QUALITY

Since the release in 1987 of EPA reports that designated indoor air pollution as a top environmental risk to public heath, assessing and managing indoor pollutants have become the focus of integrated governmental and private efforts. In addition to health and liability concerns, productivity gains are driving improvements in indoor environmental quality. Employees' salaries are a significant cost in any commercial building, so it makes good business sense to keep staff healthy, alert, and productive.

The LEED for Commercial Interiors Rating System aims to provide optimal indoor environmental quality through the careful use of technologies and strategies that improve system effectiveness and occupant productivity. For example, credits in the IEQ category encourage automatic sensors and individual controls that allow users to adjust temperature, humidity, and ventilation based on individual preference.

Ensuring excellent indoor environmental quality requires systems and occupants to work in sync, which in turn requires the joint efforts of the building owner, tenant, design team, contractors, and suppliers. The LEED 2009 for Commercial Interiors Rating System focuses on providing an optimal environment for occupants by specifically addressing areas over which the tenant has control or influence. Additional issues addressed by the rating system include access to daylight, lighting quality, ventilation, thermal comfort, and access to views. These issues all have the potential to enhance the indoor environment and optimize the interior for building occupants.

SYNERGIES

This category covers two overarching concepts—maintaining high-quality indoor air and providing a high level of occupant comfort. Both of these concepts entail multiple specific strategies, such as providing access to daylight (occupant comfort) and specifying low-emitting flooring systems (air quality). While they may seem disconnected, they actually work together to maintain a healthy and productivity-enhancing indoor environment, and both concepts focus on the occupant. For example, poor daylight design may cause glare and unwanted heat gain, which would make a space thermally and visually uncomfortable. From another perspective, many interior materials and finishes contain odorous, irritating, and/or harmful contaminants that off-gas within the commercial interior and continue to do so long after they are installed.

Additionally, the credits in this category may have a significant impact on energy consumption. Occupant thermal comfort, ventilation rate, and air filtration often depend on mechanical systems. When a project includes occupant controls for lighting and thermal comfort, the project team will need to work together to assess how the controls could affect energy consumption. Furthermore, the team will need to work with suppliers, contractors, and the commissioning authority to ensure that the systems are installed and functioning as intended.

INDOOR ENVIRONMENTAL QUALITY

As you study, consider the synergies related to the Energy and Atmosphere category and the Materials and Resources category.

CATEGORY HIGHLIGHTS

- Several referenced standards are used within the Indoor Environmental Quality category. Make sure you pay attention to these standards and can remember which standard is associated with each credit.

- LEED projects must achieve minimum ventilation rates. Additional credit is awarded for projects that sufficiently exceed this minimum level.

- Construction activities and the specification of interior finish materials have lasting effects on the air quality of the space. Careful selection of low-emitting materials and conscientious construction practices are recognized in this category.

- Providing occupant controllability, access to views and daylight, increased ventilation, and superior thermal comfort are all specifically considered within this category.

INDOOR ENVIRONMENTAL QUALITY

INDOOR ENVIRONMENTAL QUALITY CREDITS

CREDIT	TITLE
IEQ Prerequisite 1	Minimum Indoor Air Quality Performance
IEQ Prerequisite 2	Environmental Tobacco Smoke (ETS) Control
IEQ Credit 1	Outdoor Air Delivery Monitoring
IEQ Credit 2	Increased Ventilation
IEQ Credit 3.1	Construction Indoor Air Quality Management Plan—During Construction
IEQ Credit 3.2	Construction Indoor Air Quality Management Plan—Before Occupancy
IEQ Credit 4.1	Low-Emitting Materials—Adhesives and Sealants
IEQ Credit 4.2	Low-Emitting Materials—Paints and Coatings
IEQ Credit 4.3	Low-Emitting Materials—Flooring Systems
IEQ Credit 4.4	Low-Emitting Materials—Composite Wood and Agrifiber Products
IEQ Credit 4.5	Low-Emitting Materials—Systems Furniture and Seating
IEQ Credit 5	Indoor Chemical and Pollutant Source Control
IEQ Credit 6.1	Controllability of Systems—Lighting
IEQ Credit 6.2	Controllability of Systems—Thermal Comfort
IEQ Credit 7.1	Thermal Comfort—Design
IEQ Credit 7.2	Thermal Comfort—Verification
IEQ Credit 8.1	Daylight and Views—Daylight
IEQ Credit 8.2	Daylight and Views—Views for Seated Spaces

IEQ

KEY TERMS

Adhesive	Any substance used to bond one surface to another by attachment. Adhesives include bonding primers, adhesive primers, and adhesive primers for plastics. (SCAQMD Rule 1168)
Aerosol adhesive	An aerosol product in which the spray mechanism is permanently housed in a nonrefillable can. Designed for hand-held application, these products do not need ancillary hoses or spray equipment. Aerosol adhesives include special-purpose spray adhesives, mist spray adhesives, and web spray adhesives. (SCAQMD Rule 1168)
Agrifiber products	Products made from agricultural fiber. Examples include particleboard, medium-density fiberboard (MDF), plywood, oriented-strand board (OSB), wheatboard, and strawboard.
Anticorrosive paints	Coatings formulated and recommended for use in preventing the corrosion of ferrous metal substrates.
Architectural porous sealant	A substance used as a sealant on porous materials.
Audiovisual (A/V)	Slides, film, video, sound recordings, and the devices used to present such media.
Building envelope	The entire outer shell of a building, including areas of walls, floors and ceilings.
Carbon dioxide (CO₂) levels	An indicator of ventilation effectiveness inside buildings. CO_2 concentrations greater than 530 ppm above outdoor CO_2 conditions generally indicate inadequate ventilation. Absolute concentrations of CO_2 greater than 800 to 1,000 ppm generally indicate poor air quality for breathing.
Coating	A coating is applied to beautify, protect, or provide a barrier to a surface. Flat coatings register a gloss of less than 15 on an 85-degree meter or less than 5 on a 60-degree meter. Nonflat coatings register a gloss of 5 or greater on a 60-degree meter and a gloss of 15 or greater on an 85-degree meter. (SCAQMD Rule 1113)
Comfort criteria	Specific design conditions that take into account temperature, humidity, air speed, outdoor temperature, outdoor humidity, seasonal clothing, and expected activity. (ASHRAE 55–2004)

Composite wood	Wood or plant particles or fibers bonded by a synthetic resin or binder. Examples include particleboard, medium-density fiberboard (MDF), plywood, oriented-strand board (OSB), wheatboard, and strawboard.
Contaminants	Unwanted airborne elements that may reduce indoor air quality. (ASHRAE 62.1– 2007)
Controls	Mechanisms that allow occupants to direct power to devices (such as lights and heaters) or adjust devices or systems within a range (such as brightness and temperature).
Core learning spaces	Areas for educational activities where the primary functions are teaching and learning. (ANSI S12.60–2002)
Densely occupied space	An area with a design occupant density of 25 people or more per 1,000 square feet (40 square feet or less per person).
Environmental tobacco smoke (ETS)	Also known as secondhand smoke, it consists of airborne particles emitted from the burning end of cigarettes, pipes, and cigars and is exhaled by smokers. These particles contain about 4,000 compounds, up to 50 of which are known to cause cancer.
Footcandle (fc)	A measure of light falling on a given surface. One footcandle is defined as the quantity of light falling on a 1 square-foot area from a 1candela light source at a distance of 1 foot (which equals 1 lumen per square foot). Footcandles can be measured both horizontally and vertically by a footcandle meter or light meter.
Formaldehyde	A naturally occurring VOC found in small amounts in animals and plants but is carcinogenic and an irritant to most people when present in high concentrations, causing headaches, dizziness, mental impairment, and other symptoms. When present in the air at levels above 0.1 ppm, it can cause watery eyes; burning sensations in the eyes, nose, and throat; nausea; coughing; chest tightness; wheezing; skin rashes; and asthmatic and allergic reactions.
Group (shared) multi-occupant spaces	Conference rooms, classrooms, and other indoor spaces used as places of congregation.
HVAC systems	Equipment, distribution systems, and terminals that provide the processes of heating, ventilating, or air conditioning. (ASHRAE 90.1– 2007)

Individual occupant spaces	Standard workstations where workers conduct individual tasks.
Indoor adhesive, sealant, or sealant primer	An adhesive or sealant product applied on-site, inside the building's weatherproofing system.
Indoor air quality (IAQ)	The nature of air inside the space that affects the health and well-being of building occupants. It is considered acceptable when there are no known contaminants at harmful concentrations and a substantial majority (80% or more) of the occupants do not express dissatisfaction. (ASHRAE 62.1–2007)
Mechanical ventilation, or active ventilation	Ventilation provided by mechanically powered equipment, such as motor-driven fans and blowers, but not by devices such as wind-driven turbine ventilators and mechanically operated windows. (ASHRAE 62.1–2004)
Minimum efficiency reporting value (MERV)	A filter rating established by the American Society of Heating, Refrigerating and Air-Conditioning Engineers (ASHRAE 52.2–1999, Method of Testing General Ventilation Air-Cleaning Devices for Removal Efficiency by Particle Size). MERV categories range from 1 (very low efficiency) to 16 (very high efficiency).
Mixed-mode ventilation	A combination of mechanical and natural ventilation methods.
Natural ventilation, or passive ventilation	Includes thermal, wind, or diffusion effects through doors, windows, or other intentional openings in the building; it uses the building layout, fabric, and form to achieve heat transfer and air movement.
Noise reduction coefficient (NRC)	The arithmetic average of absorption coefficients at 250, 500, 1,000, and 2,000 Hz for a material. The NRC is often published by manufacturers in product specifications, particularly for acoustical ceiling tiles and acoustical wall panels.
Nonoccupied spaces	All rooms used by maintenance personnel that are not open for use by occupants. Examples are closets and janitorial, storage, and equipment rooms.
Nonporous sealant	A substance used as a sealant on nonporous materials. Nonporous materials, such as plastic and metal, do not have openings in which fluids may be absorbed or discharged.

Occupants	In a commercial building, occupants are workers who either have a permanent office or workstation in the building or typically spend a minimum of 10 hours per week in the building. In a residential building, occupants also include all persons who live in the building. In schools, occupants also include students, faculty, support staff, administrators, and maintenance employees.
Off-gassing	The emission of volatile organic compounds (VOCs) from synthetic and natural products.
Outdoor air	The ambient air that enters a building through a ventilation system, either through natural ventilation or by infiltration. (ASHRAE 62.1–2007)
Ozone (O$_3$)	A gas composed of three oxygen atoms. It is not usually emitted directly into the air, but at ground level it is created by a chemical reaction between oxides of nitrogen (NOx) and volatile organic compounds (VOCs) in the presence of sunlight. Ozone has the same chemical structure whether it occurs in the atmosphere or at ground level and can have positive or negative effects, depending on its location. (U.S. Environmental Protection Agency)
Phenol formaldehyde	A chemical that off-gasses only at high temperatures, it is used for exterior products, although many of these products are suitable for interior applications.
Porous materials	Materials with tiny openings, often microscopic, that can absorb or discharge fluids. Examples include wood, fabric, paper, corrugated paperboard, and plastic foam. (SCAQMD Rule 1168)
Regularly occupied spaces	Areas where workers are seated or standing as they work inside a building. In residential applications, these areas are all spaces except bathrooms, utility areas, and closets or other storage rooms. In schools, they are areas where students, teachers, or administrators are seated or standing as they work or study inside a building.
Relative humidity	The ratio of partial density of airborne water vapor to the saturation density of water vapor at the same temperature and total pressure.
Reverberation	An acoustical phenomenon that occurs when sound persists in an enclosed space because of its repeated reflection or scattering on the enclosing surfaces or objects within the space. (ANSI S12.60–2002)

Reverberation time (RT)	A measure of the amount of reverberation in a space and equal to the time required for the level of a steady sound to decay by 60 dB after the sound has stopped. The decay rate depends on the amount of sound absorption in a room, the room geometry, and the frequency of the sound. RT is expressed in seconds. (ANSI S12.60–2002)
Sound absorption	The portion of sound energy striking a surface that is not returned as sound energy. (ANSI S12.60–2002)
Sound absorption coefficient	The ability of a material to absorb sound, expressed as a fraction of incident sound. The sound absorption coefficient is frequency specific and ranges from 0.00 to 1.00. For example, a material may have an absorption coefficient of 0.50 at 250 Hz and 0.80 at 1,000 Hz. This indicates that the material absorbs 50% of incident sound at 250 Hz and 80% of incident sound at 1,000 Hz. The arithmetic average of absorption coefficients at midfrequencies is the noise reduction coefficient.
Sound transmission class (STC)	A single-number rating for the acoustic attenuation of airborne sound passing through a partition or other building element, such as a wall, roof, or door, as measured in an acoustical testing laboratory according to accepted industry practice. A higher STC rating provides more sound attenuation through a partition. (ANSI S12.60–2002)
Thermal comfort	When occupants express satisfaction with the thermal environment.
Urea formaldehyde	A combination of urea and formaldehyde that is used in some glues and may emit formaldehyde at room temperature.
Ventilation	The process of supplying air to or removing air from a space for the purpose of controlling air contaminant levels, humidity, or temperature within the space. (ASHRAE 62.1–2007).
Visible light transmittance (VLT) (Tvis)	The ratio of total transmitted light to total incident light (that is, the amount of visible spectrum, 380–780 nanometers of light passing through a glazing surface divided by the amount of light striking the glazing surface). The higher the Tvis value, the more incident light passes through the glazing.
Vision glazing	The portion of an exterior window between 30 and 90 inches above the floor that permits a view to the outside.

Volatile organic compounds (VOCs)	Carbon compounds that participate in atmospheric photochemical reactions (excluding carbon monoxide, carbon dioxide, carbonic acid, metallic carbides and carbonates, and ammonium carbonate). The compounds vaporize (become a gas) at normal room temperatures.
Weighted decibel (dBA)	A sound pressure level measured with a conventional frequency weighting that roughly approximates how the human ear hears different frequency components of sounds at typical listening levels for speech. (ANSI S12.60–2002)

Required | **IEQ Prerequisite 1: Minimum Indoor Air Quality Performance**

5 Points | **IEQ Credit 2: Increased Ventilation**

KEY TERMS

INDOOR AIR QUALITY (IAQ)

MECHANICAL VENTILATION

MIXED-MODE VENTILATION

NATURAL VENTILATION

OUTDOOR AIR

VENTILATION

RELATED CREDITS

SS Credit 1: Option 1, Path 2, Brownfield Redevelopment

SS Credit 4: Alternative Transportation

EA Prerequisite 1: Fundamental Commissioning

EA Credit 1: Optimize Energy Performance

EA Credit 2: Enhanced Commissioning

EA Credit 3: Measurement and Verification

IEQ Prerequisite 2: Environmental Tobacco Smoke

IEQ Credit 1: Outdoor Air Delivery Monitoring

IEQ Credit 4: Low-Emitting Materials

IEQ Credit 5: Indoor Chemical and Pollutant Source Control

INTENT

IEQ Prerequisite 1:

To establish minimum indoor air quality (IAQ) performance to enhance indoor air quality in buildings, thus contributing to the comfort and well-being of the occupants.

IEQ Credit 2:

To provide additional air ventilation to improve indoor air quality for improved occupant comfort, well-being, and productivity.

REQUIREMENTS

For mechanically ventilated spaces:

IEQ Prerequisite 1:

Modify or maintain each outside air intake, supply air fan, and/or ventilation distribution system to supply at least the outdoor air ventilation rate required by ASHRAE Standard 62.1–2007.

If the project cannot meet the minimum levels of the referenced standard, document why it is not possible to supply the minimum rates and complete an engineering assessment of the system's maximum ventilation rate. Confirm that an absolute minimum of 10 cubic feet per minute per person is supplied to the space.

IEQ Credit 2:

Increase the outdoor air supply to exceed the prerequisite requirements of ASHRAE 62.1–2007 by at least 30%.

For naturally ventilated spaces:

IEQ Prerequisite 1:

Comply with ASHRAE Standard 62.1–2007, Paragraph 5.1.

If the project cannot meet the minimum levels of the referenced standard, document why it is not possible to supply the minimum rates and complete an engineering assessment of the system's maximum ventilation rate. Confirm that an absolute minimum of 10 cubic feet per minute per person is supplied to the space.

IEQ Credit 2: Increased Ventilation

REQUIREMENTS, CONTINUED

IEQ Credit 2:

Design the system to meet the recommendations of the Carbon Trust's "Good Practice Guide 237."

Additionally, follow the flow diagram process shown in Figure 1.18 of the Chartered Institute of Building Services Engineers (CIBSE) Applications Manual 10–2005, Natural Ventilation in Non-Domestic Buildings.

Finally, show that the natural ventilation will be effective by either using diagrams and calculations (showing that the design meets the CIBSE Applications Manual 10–2005 standards) or providing analytic modeling to demonstrate compliance with ASHRAE 62.1–2007, Chapter 6, in at least 90% of spaces.

IMPLEMENTATION

Design the building to meet the minimum required ventilation rates for mechanically ventilated, naturally ventilated, and mixed-mode ventilated spaces based on the referenced standard(s).

- Mechanically ventilated spaces should use the Ventilation Rate Procedure detailed in ASHRAE 62.1–2007.
- Naturally ventilated spaces should use ASHRAE Standard 62.1–2007, Paragraph 5.1.
- Mixed-mode ventilated spaces should meet the minimum ventilation rates required by Chapter 6 of ASHRAE 62.1–2007.

Projects pursuing IEQ Credit 2: Increased Ventilation, must provide an additional 30% outdoor air to all spaces with mechanical ventilation (including mixed mode). Spaces without mechanical ventilation (naturally ventilated) must be designed to meet the Carbon Trust's "Good Practice Guide 237."

DOCUMENTATION & CALCULATIONS

The mechanical designer should develop ventilation calculations demonstrating compliance with the applicable sections of ASHRAE 62.1–2007 and, where required, create diagrams and calculations or an analytic model to confirm natural ventilation effectiveness.

TIME LINE/TEAM

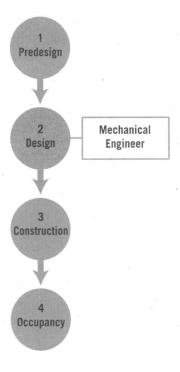

1 Predesign

2 Design — Mechanical Engineer

3 Construction

4 Occupancy

STANDARDS

ASHRAE 62.1–2007, Ventilation for Acceptable Indoor Air Quality

CIBSE Applications Manual 10–2005, Natural Ventilation in Non-Domestic Buildings

The Carbon Trust's "Good Practice Guide 237, Natural Ventilation in Non-Domestic Buildings, A Guide for Designers, Developers, and Owners," 1998

When local code is more stringent, it should be used in lieu of ASHRAE 62.1–2007.

KEY TERMS

ENVIRONMENTAL TOBACCO SMOKE
(ETS)

RELATED CREDITS

EA Prerequisite 1:
Fundamental Commissioning

EA Credit 1: Optimize Energy
Performance

EA Credit 2: Enhanced
Commissioning

EA Credit 3: Measurement and
Verification

IEQ Prerequisite 1: Minimum
Indoor Air Quality Performance

IEQ Credit 1: Outdoor Air
Delivery Monitoring

IEQ Credit 2: Increased
Ventilation

IEQ Credit 4: Low-Emitting
Materials

IEQ Credit 5: Indoor Chemical
and Pollutant Source Control

INTENT

To prevent or minimize exposure of building occupants, indoor surfaces, and ventilation air distribution systems to environmental tobacco smoke (ETS).

REQUIREMENTS

Prohibit smoking in the tenant space, all common areas, and all areas of the base building that share a ventilation system with the commercial interior. Projects may allow indoor smoking only in designated smoking rooms designed to mitigate the impacts of uncontrolled ETS.

Prohibit smoking within 25 feet of all operable windows, doors, and air intakes.

For residential and hospitality projects, in addition to the above requirements, tightly seal all penetrations and adjacent vertical chases in residential units to control ETS transfer between units, and weather-strip all doors leading to common hallways and windows and doors to the building exterior to control ETS transfer to common areas. Conduct blower door testing to demonstrate that the units are sufficiently sealed.

IMPLEMENTATION

Prohibit smoking within the tenant space.

Locate the project in a building that prohibits smoking in all common areas and other areas with shared ventilation systems. Ensure that the building has posted signage to designate smoking and nonsmoking areas, and ensure that the 25-foot setback requirements are met for all doors, operable windows, and building air intakes.

If smoking areas exist within the tenant space, install separate and isolated ventilation systems.

IMPLEMENTATION, CONTINUED

Residential and hospitality projects that allow smoking should protect other tenants from the environmental tobacco smoke using the following methods:

- Choosing very tight construction;
- Sealing any penetrations in walls, ceilings, and floors in each residential unit;
- Sealing all vertical chases adjacent to units;
- Weather-stripping all exterior doors and operable windows and in the residential units leading to common areas; and
- Conducting blower door testing according to the referenced standards.

DOCUMENTATION & CALCULATIONS

Develop an environmental tobacco smoke policy, maintaining site plans or similar documents that show where smoking is prohibited. If smoking is allowed within the building, track and record testing data for interior smoking rooms to confirm that no cross-contamination takes place.

NOTES

The relationship between smoking and various health risks, including lung disease, cancer, and heart disease, is well documented. A strong link between ETS and similar health risks has also been demonstrated.

TIME LINE/TEAM

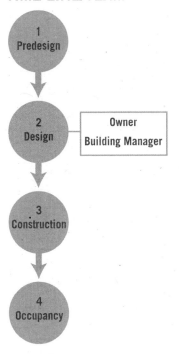

STANDARDS

American National Standards Institute (ANSI)/ASTM-E779–03, Standard Test Method for Determining Air Leakage Rate by Fan Pressurization

Residential Manual for Compliance with California's 2001 Energy Efficiency Standards (for Low Rise Residential Buildings), Chapter 4

KEY TERMS

CARBON DIOXIDE (CO_2)

DENSELY OCCUPIED SPACE

HVAC SYSTEMS

INDOOR AIR QUALITY (IAQ)

MECHANICAL VENTILATION

NATURAL VENTILATION

OUTDOOR AIR

VENTILATION

RELATED CREDITS

 SS Credit 1: Option 1, Path 2, Brownfield Redevelopment

SS Credit 3: Alternative Transportation

EA Prerequisite 1: Fundamental Commissioning

EA Credit 2: Enhanced Commissioning

EA Credit 3: Measurement and Verification

IEQ Credit 2: Increased Ventilation

INTENT

To provide capacity for ventilation system monitoring to promote occupant comfort and well-being.

REQUIREMENTS

Install CO_2 sensors that signal when carbon dioxide (CO_2) values vary by 10% or more from the design values. For densely occupied mechanically ventilated spaces and all naturally ventilated spaces, monitor CO_2 concentrations within all spaces. For ventilation systems that serve nondensely occupied spaces, install outdoor air intake measuring devices.

CO_2 sensors must be located in the area where occupants breathe (the breathing zone): 3 to 6 feet above the floor.

IMPLEMENTATION

Monitor the outdoor airflow rate as a way to confirm that HVAC equipment is providing the required ventilation rate.

CO_2 monitoring should be applied to both densely occupied mechanically ventilated and all naturally ventilated spaces.

DOCUMENTATION & CALCULATIONS

Document the CO_2 sensors and/or airflow monitors on project drawings, indicating location, and in mechanical schedules.

Incorporate the systems into the commissioning process.

NOTES

HVAC systems are designed to flush out indoor airborne contaminants, so why wouldn't you want to monitor them?

Nondensely occupied spaces are defined as having fewer than 25 people per 1,000 square feet.

Naturally ventilated areas that use measures to induce airflow through multiple spaces equally may be monitored together.

TIME LINE/TEAM

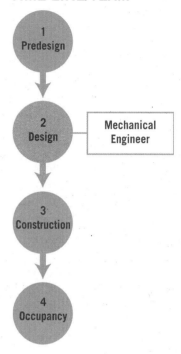

1 Predesign

2 Design — Mechanical Engineer

3 Construction

4 Occupancy

STANDARDS

ASHRAE 62.1–2007, Ventilation for Acceptable Indoor Air Quality

KEY TERMS

HVAC SYSTEMS

INDOOR AIR QUALITY (IAQ)

MINIMUM EFFICIENCY REPORTING VALUE (MERV)

RELATED CREDITS

 IEQ Credit 3.2: Construction Indoor Air Quality Management Plan – Before Occupancy

 IEQ Credit 4: Low-Emitting Materials

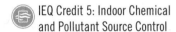 IEQ Credit 5: Indoor Chemical and Pollutant Source Control

INTENT

To reduce indoor air quality (IAQ) problems resulting from construction or renovation and promote the comfort and well-being of construction workers and building occupants.

REQUIREMENTS

Create an IAQ management plan for the construction and preoccupancy phases.

During construction, meet or exceed the Sheet Metal and Air Conditioning Contractors National Association's (SMACNA) control measures.

Protect stored on-site or installed absorptive materials from moisture damage.

If permanently installed air handlers are used during construction, MERV 8 filtration media must be used at each return air grille. Replace all filtration media immediately prior to occupancy.

IMPLEMENTATION

Create an IAQ management plan to guide the construction and preoccupancy IAQ management practices. Educate and review the plan with subcontractors and field personnel to ensure implementation.

The IAQ management plan should address the following:

- Storage of construction materials in order to avoid moisture damage;
- Installation of filters if air handlers will be used during construction;
- HVAC protection;
- Source control;
- Pathway interruption;
- Housekeeping; and
- Scheduling.

DOCUMENTATION & CALCULATIONS

Develop a construction indoor air quality management plan.

Take photos to log IAQ management plan practices.

NOTES

Building construction has the potential to introduce contaminants, such as dust, into the building. If unaddressed, the contamination can result in poor indoor air quality extending over the lifetime of the building.

TIME LINE/TEAM

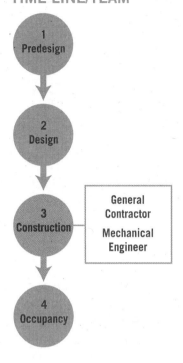

STANDARDS

Sheet Metal and Air Conditioning Contractors National Association (SMACNA) IAQ Guidelines for Occupied Buildings Under Construction, 2nd Edition 2007, ANSI/SMACNA 008-2008 (Chapter 3)

ANSI/ASHRAE Standard 52.2–1999, Method of Testing General Ventilation Air-Cleaning Devices for Removal Efficiency by Particle Size

KEY TERMS

CONTAMINANTS

HVAC SYSTEMS

INDOOR AIR QUALITY (IAQ)

OUTDOOR AIR

RELATED CREDITS

 IEQ Prerequisite 1: Minimum Indoor Air Quality Performance

 IEQ Credit 2: Increased Ventilation

 IEQ Credit 3.1: Construction Indoor Air Quality Management Plan – During Construction

 IEQ Credit 4: Low-Emitting Materials

 IEQ Credit 5: Indoor Chemical and Pollutant Source Control

INTENT

To reduce indoor air quality (IAQ) problems resulting from construction or renovation and promote the comfort and well-being of workers and occupants.

REQUIREMENTS

Either complete a tenant space flush-out to remove contaminants or conduct air quality testing to confirm that contaminants are below allowable levels.

Flush-Out:

Conduct a flush-out that supplies 14,000 cubic feet of outside air per square foot to the project interior. If occupancy is desired prior to completion, the space may be occupied after 3,500 cubic feet of outside air per square foot have been delivered, as long as acceptable minimum ventilation rates are maintained until the full flush-out (14,000 cubic feet per square foot) has been completed.

IAQ Testing:

Conduct air quality testing prior to occupancy to confirm that indoor air contaminants are within the following thresholds:

Contaminant	Maximum Concentration
Formaldehyde	27 parts per billion
Particulates (PM10)	50 micrograms per cubic meter
Total volatile organic compounds (TVOCs)	500 micrograms per cubic meter
4-Phenylcyclohexene (4-PCH)*	6.5 micrograms per cubic meter
Carbon monoxide (CO)	9 parts per million and no greater than 2 parts per million above outdoor levels
*This test is required only if carpets and fabrics with styrene butadiene rubber [SBR] latex backing are installed as part of the base building systems.	

IMPLEMENTATION

Complete all construction-related and cleaning activities prior to flush-out or air quality testing.

Flush-Out Procedure:

- Install new filtration media and flush out the space.

IMPLEMENTATION, CONTINUED

- Supply a total outdoor air volume of 14,000 cubic feet per square foot of floor area while maintaining an internal temperature of at least 60 F and maintaining a relative humidity no higher than 60%.
- The space may be occupied after at least 3,500 cubic feet of outdoor air per square foot of floor area have been delivered and the space has been ventilated at a minimum rate of 0.30 cfm per square foot of outdoor air or the design minimum outside air rate (whichever is greater).
  - Continue the flush-out until the total of 14,000 cubic feet per square foot of outdoor air has been delivered to the space.
- The flush-out may continue during occupancy.

Air Quality Testing:

- This approach confirms that major contaminants are below the acceptable level.
- Avoid substitutions for low-emitting materials.
- Use low-VOC cleaning supplies.
- Use vacuum cleaners with HEPA filters.
- Use the protocol outlined in the referenced standard.
  - Select appropriate sampling locations.
  - Take at least one sample per 25,000 square feet.
  - Take samples in the breathing zone and during normal occupied hours.
- Record exact sample locations in case retesting is required.
- Pass the test! If you don't, flush out the space and retest.
  - Retesting may be limited to only those contaminants that exceed the maximum levels.

DOCUMENTATION & CALCULATIONS

- For projects completing a flush-out procedure, record the procedures, including start date and time. Confirm how humidity and temperature requirements will be met.
- For projects completing air quality testing, record the testing procedures, including the sampling locations. Document the air contaminant values as measured.

NOTES

Construction has the potential to introduce contaminants into the project interior. To prevent poor indoor air quality over the lifetime of the building, institute IAQ management strategies to minimize contaminants.

TIME LINE/TEAM

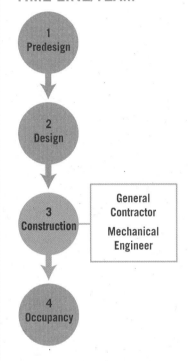

1 Predesign

2 Design

3 Construction — General Contractor / Mechanical Engineer

4 Occupancy

STANDARDS

U.S. Environmental Protection Agency Compendium of Methods for the Determination of Air Pollutants in Indoor Air

1 Point

IEQ Credit 4.1: Low-Emitting Materials – Adhesives and Sealants

KEY TERMS

ADHESIVE

AEROSOL ADHESIVE

CONTAMINANTS

INDOOR AIR QUALITY (IAQ)

OCCUPANTS

OFF-GASSING

VOLATILE ORGANIC COMPOUNDS (VOCS)

RELATED CREDITS

 IEQ Prerequisite 2: Environmental Tobacco Smoke (ETS) Control

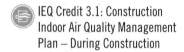 IEQ Credit 3.1: Construction Indoor Air Quality Management Plan – During Construction

 IEQ Credit 3.2: Construction Indoor Air Quality Management Plan – Before Occupancy

IEQ Credit 4.2: Low-Emitting Materials – Paints and Coatings

IEQ Credit 4.3: Low-Emitting Materials – Flooring Systems

IEQ Credit 4.4: Low-Emitting Materials – Composite Wood and Agrifiber Products

IEQ Credit 4.5: Low-Emitting Materials – Systems Furniture and Seating

IEQ Credit 5: Indoor Chemical and Pollutant Source Control

INTENT

To reduce the quantity of indoor air contaminants that are odorous, potentially irritating, and/or harmful to the comfort and well-being of installers and occupants.

REQUIREMENTS

Adhesives, sealants, and sealant primers installed in the project interior must comply with South Coast Air Quality Management District (SCAQMD) Rule 1168.

Aerosol adhesives must comply with the Green Seal Standard for Commercial Adhesives GS-36 requirements.

IMPLEMENTATION

Include VOC limits or identify specific products within the project specifications.

DOCUMENTATION & CALCULATIONS

Track all indoor aerosol adhesive products, adhesives, sealants, and sealant primers used in the project.

The VOC budget methodology compares the design case with a baseline case in order to demonstrate that the overall low-VOC performance has been attained. When the design is less than the baseline, the credit requirement is satisfied. If a product with higher than allowable VOC content is used, follow the VOC budget approach to determine whether the credit can still be achieved.

NOTES

The VOC threshold limits and content are generally expressed in grams per liter (g/L).

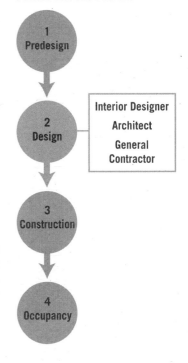

TIME LINE/TEAM

1 Predesign

2 Design — Interior Designer / Architect / General Contractor

3 Construction

4 Occupancy

STANDARDS

South Coast Air Quality Management District (SCAQMD) Amendment to South Coast Rule 1168, VOC Limits, effective January 7, 2005

Green Seal Standard 36 (GS-36), effective October 19, 2000

KEY TERMS

ANTICORROSIVE PAINTS

COATING

CONTAMINANTS

INDOOR AIR QUALITY (IAQ)

OCCUPANTS

VOLATILE ORGANIC COMPOUNDS
(VOCS)

RELATED CREDITS

 IEQ Prerequisite 2:
Environmental Tobacco Smoke
(ETS) Control

IEQ Credit 3.1: Construction
Indoor Air Quality Management
Plan – During Construction

IEQ Credit 3.2: Construction
Indoor Air Quality Management
Plan – Before Occupancy

IEQ Credit 4.1: Low-Emitting
Materials – Adhesives and
Sealants

IEQ Credit 4.3: Low-Emitting
Materials – Flooring Systems

IEQ Credit 4.4: Low-Emitting
Materials – Composite Wood
and Agrifiber Products

IEQ Credit 4.5: Low-Emitting
Materials – Systems Furniture
and Seating

IEQ Credit 5: Indoor Chemical
and Pollutant Source Control

INTENT

To reduce the quantity of indoor air contaminants that are odorous, irritating, and/or harmful to the comfort and well-being of installers and occupants.

REQUIREMENTS

Paints and coatings used in the project interior must meet the following requirements:

● Architectural paints and coatings must comply with GS-11.

● Anticorrosive and antirust paints must comply with GC-3.

● Clear wood finishes, floor coatings, stains, primers, and shellacs applied to interior elements must comply with South Coast Air Quality Management District (SCAQMD) Rule 1113.

IMPLEMENTATION

Include VOC limits or identify specific products within the project specifications.

DOCUMENTATION & CALCULATIONS

Track all paints and coatings used in the project.

The VOC budget methodology compares the design case with a baseline case in order to demonstrate that the overall low-VOC performance has been attained. When the design is less than the baseline, the credit requirement is satisfied. If a product with higher than allowable VOC content is used, follow the VOC budget approach to determine whether the credit can still be achieved.

NOTES

The VOC threshold limits and content are generally expressed in grams per liter (g/L).

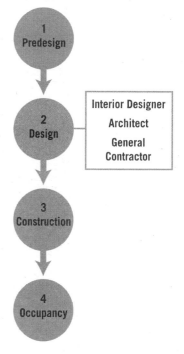

TIME LINE/TEAM

1 Predesign

2 Design — Interior Designer / Architect / General Contractor

3 Construction

4 Occupancy

STANDARDS

Green Seal Standard GS-11, Paints, First Edition, May 20, 1993

Green Seal Standard GC-3, Anti-Corrosive Paints, Second Edition, January 7, 1997

South Coast Air Quality Management District (SCAQMD) Rule 1113, Architectural Coatings, effective January 1, 2004

KEY TERMS

CONTAMINANTS

INDOOR AIR QUALITY (IAQ)

VOLATILE ORGANIC COMPOUNDS
(VOCS)

RELATED CREDITS

IEQ Prerequisite 2:
Environmental Tobacco Smoke
(ETS) Control

IEQ Credit 3.1: Construction
Indoor Air Quality Management
Plan – During Construction

IEQ Credit 3.2: Construction
Indoor Air Quality Management
Plan – Before Occupancy

IEQ Credit 4.1: Low-Emitting
Materials – Adhesives and
Sealants

IEQ Credit 4.2: Low-Emitting
Materials – Paints and
Coatings

IEQ Credit 4.4: Low-Emitting
Materials – Composite Wood
and Agrifiber Products

IEQ Credit 4.5: Low-Emitting
Materials – Systems Furniture
and Seating

IEQ Credit 5: Indoor Chemical
and Pollutant Source Control

INTENT

To reduce the quantity of indoor air contaminants that are odorous,
irritating, and/or harmful to the comfort and well-being of installers and
occupants.

REQUIREMENTS

All flooring installed in the interior must comply with the following
requirements as applicable to the project scope:

- All carpet must meet The Carpet and Rug Institute Green Label Plus
program requirements.

- All carpet cushion must meet The Carpet and Rug Institute Green
Label program requirements.

- All carpet adhesive must meet the requirements of IEQ Credit 4.1:
Low-Emitting Materials - Adhesives and Sealants (VOC limit of 50
g/L).

- All hard surface flooring must be certified as compliant with the
FloorScore standard.

- Concrete, wood, bamboo, and cork floor finishes must meet the
requirements of South Coast Air Quality Management District
(SCAQMD) Rule 1113, Architectural Coatings.

- Tile setting adhesives and grout must meet the requirements of
SCAQMD Rule 1168.

OR

All flooring products must meet the testing and product requirements
of the California Department of Public Health Standard Practice for the
Testing of Volatile Organic Emissions from Various Sources Using Small-
Scale Environmental Chambers, including 2004 Addenda.

IMPLEMENTATION

Include certification requirements and VOC limits and/or identify specific
products within the project specifications.

DOCUMENTATION & CALCULATIONS

Track all carpet, carpet cushion, carpet adhesive, hard surface flooring, tile setting adhesive, finishes, and grout used in the project.

NOTES

Flooring products covered by FloorScore include vinyl, linoleum, laminate flooring, wood flooring, ceramic flooring, rubber flooring, and wall base.

The VOC threshold limits and content are generally expressed in grams per liter (g/L).

TIME LINE/TEAM

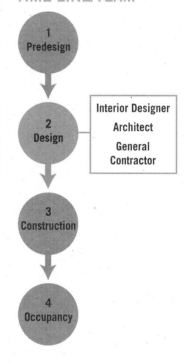

STANDARDS

The Carpet and Rug Institute (CRI) Green Label Plus Testing Program

South Coast Air Quality Management District (SCAQMD) Rule 1168, VOC Limits

SCAQMD Rule 1113, Architectural Coatings

FloorScore™ Program

California Department of Health Services Standard Practice for the Testing of Volatile Organic Emissions from Various Sources Using Small-Scale Environmental Chambers, including 2004 Addenda

KEY TERMS

AGRIFIBER PRODUCT

COMPOSITE WOOD

CONTAMINANTS

FORMALDEHYDE

INDOOR AIR QUALITY (IAQ)

OFF-GASSING

UREA-FORMALDEHYDE

RELATED CREDITS

 IEQ Prerequisite 2:
Environmental Tobacco Smoke
(ETS) Control

IEQ Credit 3.1: Construction
Indoor Air Quality Management
Plan – During Construction

IEQ Credit 3.2: Construction
Indoor Air Quality Management
Plan – Before Occupancy

IEQ Credit 4.1: Low-Emitting
Materials – Adhesives and
Sealants

 IEQ Credit 4.2: Low-Emitting
Materials – Paints and
Coatings

 IEQ Credit 4.3: Low-Emitting
Materials – Flooring Systems

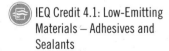 IEQ Credit 4.5: Low-Emitting
Materials – Systems Furniture
and Seating

IEQ Credit 5: Indoor Chemical
and Pollutant Source Control

INTENT

To reduce the quantity of indoor air contaminants that are odorous,
irritating, and/or harmful to the comfort and well-being of installers and
occupants.

REQUIREMENTS

Composite wood and agrifiber products used within the interior must
contain no added urea-formaldehyde resins.

Laminate adhesives used to fabricate on-site- and shop-applied composite
wood and agrifiber assemblies must not contain added urea-formaldehyde
resins.

IMPLEMENTATION

Include requirements or identify specific products within the project
specifications.

DOCUMENTATION & CALCULATIONS

Track all composite wood and agrifiber products installed in the project, and retain documentation confirming that they contain no added urea-formaldehyde resins.

NOTES

Composite wood and agrifiber products are defined as particleboard, medium-density fiberboard (MDF), plywood, wheatboard, strawboard, panel substrates, and door cores. Products covered by IEQ Credit 4.5, Low-Emitting Materials, Systems Furniture and Seating, are excluded from these requirements.

TIME LINE/TEAM

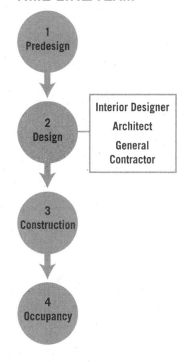

1 Predesign

2 Design — Interior Designer / Architect / General Contractor

3 Construction

4 Occupancy

STANDARDS

None

1 Point

IEQ Credit 4.5: Low-Emitting Materials – Systems Furniture and Seating

KEY TERMS

CONTAMINANTS

INDOOR AIR QUALITY (IAQ)

OFF-GASSING

VOLATILE ORGANIC COMPOUNDS (VOCS)

RELATED CREDITS

IEQ Prerequisite 2: Environmental Tobacco Smoke (ETS) Control

IEQ Credit 3.1: Construction Indoor Air Quality Management Plan – During Construction

IEQ Credit 3.2: Construction Indoor Air Quality Management Plan – Before Occupancy

IEQ Credit 4.1: Low-Emitting Materials – Adhesives and Sealants

IEQ Credit 4.2: Low-Emitting Materials – Paints and Coatings

IEQ Credit 4.3: Low-Emitting Materials – Flooring Systems

IEQ Credit 4.4: Low-Emitting Materials – Composite Wood and Agrifiber Products

IEQ Credit 5: Indoor Chemical and Pollutant Source Control

INTENT

To reduce the quantity of indoor air contaminants that are odorous, irritating, and/or harmful to the comfort and well-being of installers and occupants.

REQUIREMENTS

All systems furniture and seating must meet one of the following three options:

Option 1:

Furniture and seating are GREENGUARD Indoor Air Quality certified.

Option 2:

Calculated indoor air concentrations are less than or equal to those listed below, as determined by a procedure based on the EPA Environmental Technology Verification (ETV) Large Chamber Test Protocol for Measuring Emissions of VOCs and Aldehydes (September 1999) testing protocol conducted by an independent testing laboratory.

Option 3:

Calculated indoor air concentrations are less than or equal to those established below for furniture systems and seating, as determined by a procedure based on ANSI/BIFMA M7.1–2007 and ANSI/BIFMA X7.1–2007 testing protocol conducted by an independent testing laboratory.

IMPLEMENTATION

Specify only those materials that meet the requirements of one of the referenced standards.

DOCUMENTATION & CALCULATIONS

Track all new furniture installed in the project and retain documentation to confirm that it meets one of the three eligibility criteria.

NOTES

- Systems furniture may be either a panel-based workstation or a freestanding grouping of furniture items whose components have been designed to work in concert.

- Seating covered by this credit is defined as task and guest chairs used with systems furniture.

- Work tools attached to systems furniture are not included in the credit requirement.

- Other furniture is considered occasional furniture and does not need to be included.

- Salvaged and used furniture that is more than one year old at the time of occupancy is excluded from the credit.

- The requirement in Section 5 of ANSI/BIFMA X7.1–2007 is waived for LEED purposes. Section 5 requires that laboratories used to perform the emissions testing and/or provide analytical results must be independently accredited to ISO/IEC 17025, "general requirements for the competence of testing and calibration laboratories."

TIME LINE/TEAM

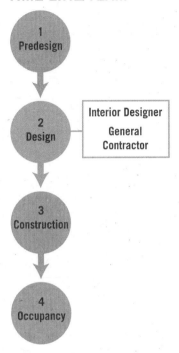

STANDARDS

ANSI/BIFMA X7.1–2007, Standard for Formaldehyde and TVOC Emissions of Low-Emitting Office Furniture Systems and Seating

Environmental Technology Verification (ETV) Large Chamber Test Protocol for Measuring Emissions of VOCs and Aldehydes, effective September 1999, U.S. EPA

GREENGUARD Certification Program

KEY TERMS

INDOOR AIR QUALITY (IAQ)

MINIMUM EFFICIENCY REPORTING VALUE (MERV)

REGULARLY OCCUPIED SPACES

RELATED CREDITS

EA Prerequisite 1: Fundamental Commissioning

EA Prerequisite 2: Minimum Energy Performance

EA Credit 1.3: Optimize Energy Performance – HVAC

EA Credit 2: Enhanced Commissioning

IEQ Prerequisite 1: Minimum Indoor Air Quality Performance

IEQ Credit 1: Outdoor Air Delivery Monitoring

IEQ Credit 3.1: Construction Indoor Air Quality Management Plan – During Construction

IEQ Credit 3.2: Construction Indoor Air Quality Management Plan – Before Occupancy

INTENT

To minimize building occupant exposure to potentially hazardous particulates, biological contaminants, and chemical pollutants that degrade air and water quality.

REQUIREMENTS

- Use entryway systems at least 10 feet long in the direction of travel at all regularly used entrances.

- Exhaust all hazardous chemical storage and use areas.

- Install MERV 13 or higher filters in mechanical ventilation systems.

- Provide appropriate containment for appropriate disposal of hazardous liquid waste.

IMPLEMENTATION

- Incorporate entryway systems at all high-traffic entrances.

- Locate and physically separate chemical storage areas (including areas with high-volume copy, print, and fax equipment) in enclosed rooms away from regularly occupied adjacent spaces, and equip these areas with a dedicated exhaust system.

- Design the mechanical system to accommodate MERV 13 filtration, and install new filters immediately prior to occupancy.

- In areas where chemical concentrate mixing occurs (such as housekeeping areas and science laboratories), install appropriate liquid waste containment.

DOCUMENTATION & CALCULATIONS

Identify the entryway systems on floor plans and reference the individual entryway systems to a listing. Also, identify all rooms or areas where chemical use is anticipated.

NOTES

If roll-out mats are used in lieu of permanent entryway systems, contract with a service organization to maintain the mats on a weekly basis.

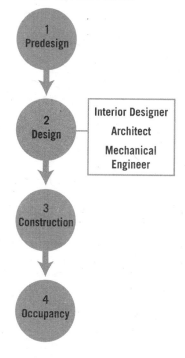

TIME LINE/TEAM

1 Predesign

2 Design — Interior Designer / Architect / Mechanical Engineer

3 Construction

4 Occupancy

STANDARDS

ANSI/ASHRAE Standard 52.2–1999, Method of Testing General Ventilation Air-Cleaning Devices for Removal Efficiency by Particle Size

1 Point

IEQ Credit 6.1:
Controllability of Systems – Lighting

KEY TERMS

CONTROLS

GROUP MULTI-OCCUPANT SPACES

INDIVIDUAL OCCUPANT SPACES

NONOCCUPIED SPACE

RELATED CREDITS

EA Prerequisite 1:
Fundamental Commissioning

EA Prerequisite 2: Minimum
Energy Performance

EA Credit 1.1: Optimize Energy
Performance – Lighting Power

EA Credit 1.2: Optimize Energy
Performance – Lighting
Controls

EA Credit 2: Enhanced
Commissioning

IEQ Credit 6.2: Controllability
of Systems – Thermal Comfort

IEQ Credit 8: Daylight and
Views

INTENT

To provide a high level of lighting system control for individual occupants or groups in multi-occupant spaces (such as classrooms and conference areas) and promote their productivity, comfort, and well-being.

REQUIREMENTS

Install individual lighting controls for at least 90% of occupants and provide group lighting controls for all shared multi-occupant spaces.

IMPLEMENTATION

Lighting controls in multi-occupant spaces must be sufficient to enable adjustments to meet the needs and preferences of the occupants.

Ninety percent or more of the occupants located at work spaces intended for individual use must have task lighting.

DOCUMENTATION & CALCULATIONS

Maintain a list of lighting controls by space type, confirming that all multi-occupant spaces have suitable controllability.

To determine how many individual lighting controls are necessary, multiply the number of workstations by 90%.

NOTES

Occupants who have control over their environment are more comfortable in a space.

TIME LINE/TEAM

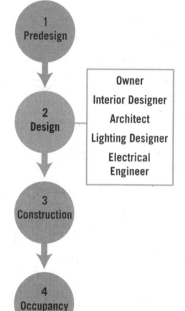

1 Predesign

2 Design

Owner
Interior Designer
Architect
Lighting Designer
Electrical Engineer

3 Construction

4 Occupancy

STANDARDS

None

1 Point

KEY TERMS

COMFORT CRITERIA

CONTROLS

GROUP (SHARED) MULTI-OCCUPANT SPACES

HVAC SYSTEMS

INDIVIDUAL OCCUPANT SPACES

NATURAL VENTILATION

NONOCCUPIED SPACES

REGULARLY OCCUPIED SPACES

THERMAL COMFORT

RELATED CREDITS

EA Prerequisite 1: Fundamental Commissioning

EA Prerequisite 2: Minimum Energy Performance

EA Credit 1.3: Optimize Energy Performance – HVAC

EA Credit 2: Enhanced Commissioning

EA Credit 3: Measurement and Verification

IEQ Credit 6.1: Controllability of Systems – Lighting

IEQ Credit 8: Daylight and Views

INTENT

To provide a high level of thermal comfort system control for individual occupants or groups in multi-occupant spaces (such as classrooms and conference areas) and promote their productivity, comfort, and well-being.

REQUIREMENTS

- Install comfort controls for at least 50% of building occupants.
- Provide comfort system controls for all shared multi-occupant spaces.

IMPLEMENTATION

- Provide individuals and groups the ability to adjust their thermal environment within the space.
- Design the comfort systems so that 50% (or more) of individual workstations have thermal comfort controls. Confirm that all shared multi-occupant spaces have thermal comfort control.

DOCUMENTATION & CALCULATIONS

Maintain a list of thermal comfort controls per space type.

To determine how many individual thermal comfort controls are necessary, multiply the number of workstations by 50%.

NOTES

Thermal comfort controllability is defined as control over one or more of the primary thermal comfort factors (air temperature, radiant temperature, air speed, or humidity).

Operable windows can be used instead of controls for workstations located 20 feet inside and no more than 10 feet to either side of the window if they meet the requirements of ASHRAE 62.1–2007, Paragraph 5.1, Natural Ventilation.

TIME LINE/TEAM

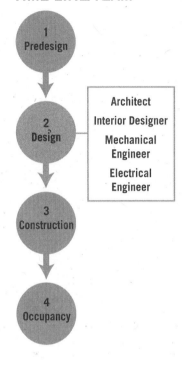

1 Predesign

2 Design

3 Construction

4 Occupancy

Architect
Interior Designer
Mechanical Engineer
Electrical Engineer

STANDARDS

ASHRAE 62.1–2007, Ventilation for Acceptable Indoor Air Quality

ASHRAE 55–2004, Thermal Environmental Conditions for Human Occupancy

| 1 Point | IEQ Credit 7.1:
Thermal Comfort – Design |

INTENT

To provide a comfortable thermal environment that promotes occupant productivity and well-being.

REQUIREMENTS

Design the HVAC system to comply with ASHRAE 55–2004.

IMPLEMENTATION

The HVAC designer evaluates the anticipated occupants within the space and designs the heating, cooling, and ventilation strategies accordingly. The activity level and attire of the occupants directly affect how comfortable people are within a given environment. It is important for the designer to consider all six primary comfort factors when designing a comfortable building. The six factors are as follows:

- Metabolic rate (activity level);
- Clothing insulation;
- Air temperature;
- Radiant temperature;
- Air speed; and
- Humidity.

Additional considerations include seasonal setpoint recommendations, change-over schedules, maintenance and operation instructions, and a maintenance and inspection schedule.

DOCUMENTATION & CALCULATIONS

The owner's project requirements and the mechanical engineer's basis of design should be reflected in design plans.

NOTES

None

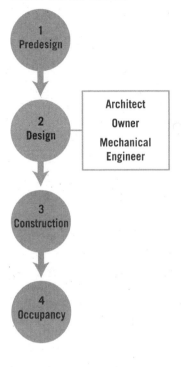

TIME LINE/TEAM

1 Predesign

2 Design — Architect / Owner / Mechanical Engineer

3 Construction

4 Occupancy

STANDARDS

ASHRAE 55–2004, Thermal Environmental Conditions for Human Occupancy

1 Point | **IEQ Credit 7.2:**
Thermal Comfort – Verification

INTENT

To provide for the assessment of occupant thermal comfort over time.

REQUIREMENTS

- Conduct an anonymous thermal comfort survey of building occupants within 6 to 18 months after the building has been occupied and develop a plan for corrective action.

- Provide a permanent monitoring system to measure and record environmental variables.

IMPLEMENTATION

- Create and administer a survey about thermal comfort conditions in person, over the phone, over networked computers, or on paper.

- Have in place a plan for corrective action.

- Install metering equipment to record environmental variables.

DOCUMENTATION & CALCULATIONS

Save a copy of the thermal comfort survey, and document the plan for corrective action.

NOTES

To be eligible for this credit, the LEED project must earn IEQ Credit 7.1: Thermal Comfort – Design.

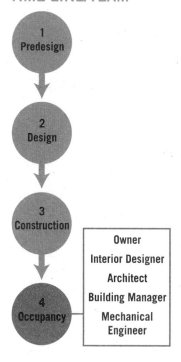

TIME LINE/TEAM

1 Predesign

2 Design

3 Construction

4 Occupancy

Owner
Interior Designer
Architect
Building Manager
Mechanical Engineer

STANDARDS

ASHRAE 55–2004, Thermal Environmental Conditions for Human Occupancy

KEY TERMS

FOOTCANDLE

REGULARLY OCCUPIED SPACE

VISIBLE LIGHT TRANSMITTANCE

VISION GLAZING

RELATED CREDITS

 EA Credit 1.1: Optimize Energy
Performance – Lighting Power

EA Credit 1.2: Optimize Energy
Performance – Lighting
Controls

EA Credit 1.3: Optimize Energy
Performance – HVAC

 IEQ Credit 6: Controllability of
Systems

IEQ Credit 8.2: Daylight and
Views – Views for Seated
Spaces

INTENT

To provide occupants with a connection between indoor spaces and the
outdoors through the introduction of daylight and views into the regularly
occupied areas of the tenant space.

REQUIREMENTS

Achieve daylight in 75% (one point) or 90% (two points) of regularly
occupied spaces. Adequate daylight can be demonstrated by any of the
following methods:

Option 1: Through computer simulation, show that the spaces are daylit
between 25 and 500 footcandles.

Option 2: Use a prescriptive approach to determine the daylight zone. The
calculation differs for side-lighting and top-lighting daylight zones.

Option 3: Take physical measurements to show that indoor daylight is at
least 25 footcandles.

Option 4: Use a combination of the above options.

IMPLEMENTATION

Consider the building geometry and further enhance daylighting through
strategic placement of windows, skylights, and light shelves.

Select glazing that will increase daylighting for occupants, and consider
glare-control options for maximum controllability.

For daylighting, provide sunlight redirection and/or glare-control devices.

The prescriptive daylighting strategies are often the hardest to understand.

For Side-Lighting Daylight Zone:

● The window-to-floor ratio multiplied by the visible light transmittance
must be between 0.150 and 0.180 to qualify.
● Only window areas above 30 inches can count in the calculation.
● The ceiling obstruction rules sound complicated, but they're pretty
simple: If a portion of the ceiling obstructs the entrance of daylight,
that related floor area must be excluded from the compliant floor area.

IMPLEMENTATION, CONTINUED

For Top-Lighting Daylight Zone:

- The daylight zone under a skylight is the outline of the opening beneath the skylight plus, in each direction, the lesser of these three options:

  - Seventy percent of the ceiling height;
  - One-half the distance to the edge of the nearest skylight (to prevent double counting of floor area from multiple skylights); or
  - The distance to any permanent opaque partition (such as a built-in bookshelf) farther away than 70% of the distance between the top of the partition and the ceiling.

- Roof skylights must cover between 3% and 6% of the roof area, the distance between the skylights must be no more than 1.4 times the ceiling height, and the glazing must have a minimum 0.5 VLT.
- If a skylight diffuser is used, it must have a measured haze value of greater than 90%.

DOCUMENTATION & CALCULATIONS

Include floor plans, sections, and elevations showing daylighting strategies and the glare-control methods used in the project.

If using daylight simulation, update the computer model as the design progresses, and create a final report summarizing the simulation results.

NOTES

Glare control is required for daylighting to prevent discomfort or disability due to glare. It also helps regulate heat gain due to sunlight.

TIME LINE/TEAM

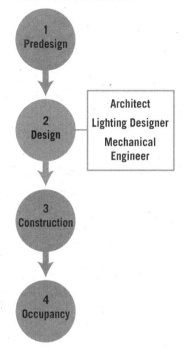

1 Predesign

2 Design — Architect / Lighting Designer / Mechanical Engineer

3 Construction

4 Occupancy

STANDARDS

ASTM D1003-07E1, Standard Test Method for Haze and Luminous Transmittance of Transparent Plastics

KEY TERMS

REGULARLY OCCUPIED SPACE

VISION GLAZING

RELATED CREDITS

 EA Credit 1.2: Optimize Energy Performance – Lighting Controls

 EA Credit 1.3: Optimize Energy Performance – HVAC

 IEQ Credit 8.1: Daylight and Views – Daylight

INTENT

To provide the building occupants a connection to the outdoors through the introduction of daylight and views into the regularly occupied areas of the tenant space.

REQUIREMENTS

Provide views to the exterior for 90% of all regularly occupied spaces.

IMPLEMENTATION

Locate open seating areas near the exterior to maximize views for all occupants. Provide glazing for core offices and multi-occupant spaces to enhance views.

A direct line of sight must be through vision glazing between 30 and 90 inches above the floor.

Draw it out:

- Sketch a line of sight at 42 inches (typical seated eye height) across the section (looking at it from the side), to establish eye height and any obstruction of the perimeter glazing.

- In plan view (looking at it from above), the area is within sight lines drawn from perimeter vision glazing.

- Double windows count too: The line of sight can be drawn through interior glazing as long as the occupant can see out another window.

- The compliant area depends on the space use type, as follows:
  - ○ Private offices: The entire square footage of the office is counted if more than 75% of the area has a direct line of sight.
  - ○ Multi-occupant spaces: Include only the actual square footage with a direct line of sight.

DOCUMENTATION & CALCULATIONS

Show locations of regularly occupied spaces with views, and maintain a spreadsheet documenting the view area.

NOTES

Regularly occupied spaces include office spaces, conference rooms, and cafeterias. Nonregularly occupied areas include support areas for copying, storage, mechanical equipment, laundry, and restrooms.

TIME LINE/TEAM

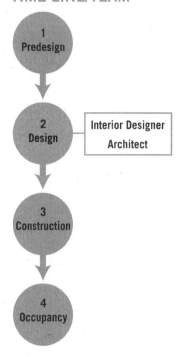

1 Predesign

2 Design — Interior Designer / Architect

3 Construction

4 Occupancy

STANDARDS

None

IEQ CATEGORY REVIEW

1 How should optimal ventilation rates be determined for a project?

_____

_____

2 What factors determine how comfortable people are within an indoor environment?

_____

_____

3 List items that will be addressed in an effective IAQ management plan during the construction phase:

_____

_____

4 What are major sources of pollution in buildings and what are some potential strategies to manage them?

_____

_____

5 What building attributes should design teams take into account when assessing daylight and views?

_____

_____

Walk through an office or retail space in your community and identify features that affect indoor environmental quality.

List the current state of each feature as effective, neutral, ineffective or absent.

FEATURE	EFFECTIVE	NEUTRAL	INEFFECTIVE	ABSENT
Daylighting				
Ventilation				
Operable windows				
Occupant control of lighting				
Occupant control of temperature				
Low-emitting materials				
High-efficiency air filters				
Green cleaning products and technologies				
Other				

WALK AROUND

1. Identify the manufacturer of the furniture in your office; is it GREENGUARD certified? Has the furniture been tested for emissions?

2. Determine the MERV ratings of air filters in the HVAC system in your work building.

3. Determine the VOC content of all cleaning products used in the commercial interior where you work.

INVESTIGATE

Sketch the floor plan of your office, place of work, or other space where you spend time on a regular basis. Following the prescriptive option (Option 2) of IEQ Credit 8.1: Daylight and Views – Daylight, determine whether your working area meets the prescriptive requirements as a daylit space. To address any possible unknown values (such as the visible transmittance of windows, specific floor or window areas, and so on), reasonable assumptions should be made.

THINK ABOUT IT

1 When should indoor air quality testing be completed?

    a) Upon sealing the exterior envelope

    b) Before porous surfaces have been sealed

    c) During functional testing

    d) After all punch-list items have been completed

    e) Immediately following initial occupancy

 2 IEQ Credit 4.5: Low-Emitting Materials – Systems Furniture and Seating, requires that all systems furniture and seating (manufactured, refurbished, or refinished within one year prior to occupancy) meet one of three options. The three options are meeting the EPA Environmental Technology Verification Large Chamber Test Protocol for Measuring Emissions of VOCs and Aldehydes, demonstrating that emission limits from systems furniture and seating are met, or _____.

    a) Containing no added urea formaldehyde and having adhesives, sealants, paints, and coatings that are compliant with IEQ Credit 4, Low-Emitting Materials.

    b) Being GREENGUARD Indoor Air Quality certified.

    c) Being made from 100% postconsumer recycled content.

    d) Being installed prior to the building flush-out.

 3 A project team is considering pursuit of IEQ Credit 2: Increased Ventilation. Which factors should be considered to determine whether this credit is appropriate for the project? (Select two.)

    a) Estimated impact on energy use

    b) Added first cost for extra controls

    c) Improved air quality for occupants

    d) Effect on thermal comfort controls

4 A LEED for Commercial Interiors project team that is pursuing IEQ Credit 4.1: Low-Emitting Materials – Adhesives and Sealants, discovers that a subcontractor has inadvertently used a small quantity of noncompliant contact adhesive. The product has a VOC content of 85 grams per liter, while the credit threshold is 80 grams per liter. How should the team proceed?

    a) Forgo pursuit of IEQ Credit 4.1.

    b) Complete a VOC budget calculation.

    c) Submit a Credit Interpretation Request.

    d) Conduct a precompletion interior flush-out.

5 A LEED for Commercial Interiors project decides that it will prohibit smoking in the building. What else must be done to meet the requirements of IEQ Prerequisite 2: Environmental Tobacco Smoke (ETS) Control?

a) Locate in a building that prohibits smoking within 25 feet of building openings.

b) Locate in a building that provides dedicated smoking areas.

c) Locate in a building that prohibits smoking within 10 feet of pedestrian pathways and 15 feet of entrances.

d) Locate in a building that enforces smoking restrictions.

See Answer Key on page 202.

NOTES...

INNOVATION IN DESIGN

The Innovation in Design (ID) category recognizes projects for innovative building features and sustainable building practices and strategies. ID credits can be achieved by greatly exceeding what is required in an existing **LEED** credit or by demonstrating a considerable environmental benefit of a new strategy.

REGIONAL PRIORITY

LEED recognizes that not all land is created equal and has therefore identified distinct environmental zones based on their unique environmental issues. Regional Priority (RP) strives to provide an incentive for the achievement of credits that address geographically specific environmental priorities.

WHAT ABOUT INNOVATION AND REGIONAL PRIORITY?

How would you demonstrate the environmental benefits of an innovative interior design strategy?

If you were able to write a new credit for LEED, what would it be and why?

What is the most effective way to educate visitors to a LEED Platinum office space about the green building features and strategies used there?

Fresh Ideas

The following labels appear in the illustration:

RP CREDIT 1:
Regional Priority

ID CREDIT 1:
Innovation in Design

Evaluate products based on ISO 14040 life-cycle assessment

Divert waste generated from sources other than the project building site

Provide an educational program on environmental and human health benefits of green building

Exemplary Performance

ID CREDIT 2:
LEED® Accredited Professional (AP)

LEED AP

THE OVERVIEW

If you like to go above and beyond to achieve ever greater environmental benefits for your project, then you've come to the right place! These categories provide project teams with the opportunity to be awarded points for the following:

- Exemplary performance in the established requirements of existing LEED credits;
- Innovative performance in green building topics not specifically addressed by LEED;
- Primary project team member participation as a LEED Accredited Professional; and
- Achievement of credits that address environmental issues unique to a region.

As a general rule of thumb, ID credits for exemplary performance are awarded for doubling the credit requirements or achieving the next incremental percentage threshold. For instance, an ID credit for exemplary performance in WE Credit 1, Water Use Reduction, would require a minimum of 45% savings. The logic is that two points are awarded at 30% savings, a third point is awarded at 35%, and a fourth point is awarded at 40%, so the next logical increment is 45%.

INNOVATION IN DESIGN & REGIONAL PRIORITY

ID credits for innovative performance are awarded for strategies that demonstrate quantifiable environmental benefits. Strategies for sustainable building design and construction are constantly evolving and improving, and new technologies that improve building performance are continually introduced to the marketplace. Some examples of innovative performance ID credits are:

- Educational Outreach Program;
- Green Housekeeping;
- High Volume of Fly Ash;
- ISO 14040 Life-Cycle Assessment;
- Waste Management and Diversion Programs;
- Low-Emitting Furniture and Furnishings; and
- Organic Landscaping/Integrated Pest Management Program.

The ID credit for LEED Accredited Professional exists to support and encourage design integration on a project team. This person should serve a primary function in the application and certification process.

Additionally, the strategies explored in the LEED 2009 for Commercial Interiors Rating System have different environmental significance across the country and even within a city. Each distinct environmental region has been allocated six credits that address that region's specific prioritized environmental issues. A project that earns a Regional Priority credit automatically earns one point in addition to any points awarded for that credit. Up to four extra points can be earned in this way, with one point earned per credit.

SYNERGIES

The credits in this category require an integrative design process that addresses every category in LEED for Commercial Interiors. For ideas and strategies for ID opportunities, refer to the "Exemplary Performance" section of each credit in the reference guide and/or the "Exemplary Performance Matrix" in the appendix of this study guide. For a list of applicable RP credits, visit the Regional Priority database at www.usgbc.org.

INNOVATION IN DESIGN & REGIONAL PRIORITY

CATEGORY HIGHLIGHTS

- There are three ways to achieve ID points: exhibiting exemplary performance on existing LEED credits, implementing innovative strategies not covered elsewhere in LEED, and having a LEED Accredited Professional on the project team.

- You have to prove your case in order to be successful! The project team should write its own credit by following the format and rigors established in the LEED for Commercial Interiors Rating System and prove that the project has met the requirements of its new credit.

- You must be able to demonstrate significant and measurable environmental benefit.

- LEED ID credits are evaluated for each project. It is important to note that the award of an ID credit for one project at a specific point in time does not constitute automatic approval for a similar strategy in a future project.

INNOVATION IN DESIGN & REGIONAL PRIORITY

ID

CREDIT	TITLE
ID Credit 1	Innovation in Design
ID Credit 2	LEED® Accredited Professional

RP

CREDIT	TITLE
RP Credit 1	Regional Priority

KEY TERMS

LEED Accredited Professional (AP)	An individual who has successfully completed the LEED professional accreditation exam. Accreditation certifies that the individual has the knowledge and skills necessary to participate in the LEED application and certification process, holds a firm understanding of green building practices and principles, and is familiar with LEED requirements, resources, and processes.
Regional Priority	USGBC's regional councils, chapters, and affiliates have identified the environmental concerns that are locally most important for every region of the country. Six LEED credits that address those local priorities were selected for each region. A project that earns a Regional Priority credit will earn one bonus point in addition to any points awarded for that credit. Up to four extra points can be earned in this way.

KEY TERMS

None

RELATED CREDITS

None

INTENT

To provide design teams and projects the opportunity to achieve exceptional performance above the requirements set by the LEED Green Building Rating System and/or innovative performance in green building categories not specifically addressed by the LEED Green Building Rating System.

REQUIREMENTS

Credits can be achieved through any combination of the paths below:

Achieve significant, measurable environmental performance using a strategy not addressed in the LEED for Commercial Interiors Rating System.

Path 1: Innovation in Design (one to five points)

Identify the following in writing:

● The intent of the proposed innovation credit;
● The proposed requirements for compliance;
● The proposed submittals to demonstrate compliance; and
● The design approach (strategies) used to meet the requirement.

Path 2: Exemplary Performance (one to three points)

Achieve exemplary performance in an existing prerequisite or credit that allows exemplary performance. An exemplary performance point may be earned for achieving double the credit requirements and/or achieving the next incremental percentage threshold of an existing credit in LEED.

IMPLEMENTATION

● **Path 1:** Innovative strategies are those that are not addressed by any existing LEED credits. To qualify, a strategy must meet three basic criteria:

   ○ Demonstrate quantitative performance improvements for environmental benefit.
   ○ Comprehensively address the process or specification.
   ○ Involve a concept that is applicable to other projects and is significantly better than standard sustainable design practices.

● **Path 2:** Double the credit requirements or achieve the next incremental percentage threshold.

DOCUMENTATION & CALCULATIONS

- Document the process by which the project team has worked to develop and/or implement additional environmental benefits.

- Be prepared to make your case by explaining the proposed credit (Path 1) with the same rigor as an established LEED credit.

- Track your development and implementation process to illustrate the specific exceptional and innovative strategies used.

NOTES

- In preparing for the exam, it is important to understand the process to propose an innovation credit. Understanding how to create a new credit, following the structure of the LEED credit framework (including intent, requirements, potential strategies, and related standards), is key to creating a successful innovation credit.

- Keep thinking! New environmental building and design opportunities are continually emerging.

TIME LINE/TEAM

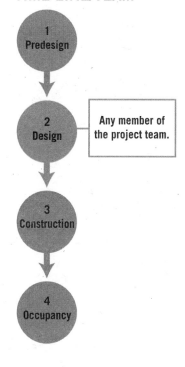

Any member of the project team.

STANDARDS

None

1 Point

ID Credit 2:
LEED® Accredited Professional (AP)

KEY TERMS

LEED ACCREDITED PROFESSIONAL
(AP)

RELATED CREDITS

None

INTENT

To support and encourage the design integration required by LEED to streamline the application and certification process.

REQUIREMENTS

At least one key project team member needs to be a LEED AP.

IMPLEMENTATION

Two options:

- Engage an individual within the organization who is already a LEED AP to participate in the application and certification process.

- Hire a LEED AP who can assist in the guidance and coordination of the LEED process.

DOCUMENTATION & CALCULATIONS

Obtain confirmation from team members who are LEED APs.

NOTES

LEED APs understand what is required to design and construct a LEED interior and how to coordinate the documentation process for LEED certification.

TIME LINE/TEAM

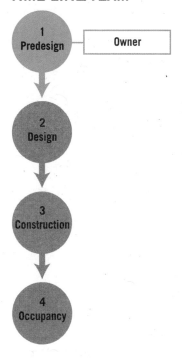

STANDARDS

LEED Accredited Professional (AP)

Green Building Certification Institute (GBCI), www.gbci.org

1 - 4 Points | **RP Credit 1:**
Regional Priority

KEY TERMS

REGIONAL PRIORITY

RELATED CREDITS

None

INTENT

To provide an incentive for the achievement of credits that address geographically specific environmental priorities.

REQUIREMENTS

Earn one to four of the six Regional Priority credits identified by the USGBC regional councils and chapters as having environmental importance for a project's region. A database of Regional Priority credits and their geographic applicability is available on the USGBC website, www.usgbc.org.

IMPLEMENTATION

Refer to the "Implementation" section under the relevant Regional Priority credit.

DOCUMENTATION & CALCULATIONS

Refer to the "Documentation Guidance" and "Calculations" sections under the relevant Regional Priority credit.

NOTES

Projects outside the United States are not eligible at this time.

TIME LINE/TEAM

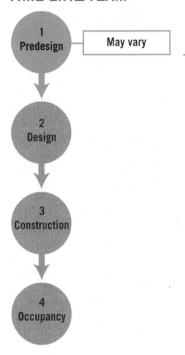

STANDARDS

Refer to the standards for a particular Regional Priority credit.

ID & RP CATEGORY REVIEW

1 Which credits can you think of that are eligible for exemplary performance? What are the requirements for achieving exemplary performance for these credits?

_____

_____

2 What strategies must you implement to achieve an Innovation in Design credit for a Green Educational Program?

_____

_____

3 What are some of the primary benefits to having a LEED AP on your project team?

_____

_____

4 List some unique environmental issues by region and note how they could be applied to credits within LEED for Commercial Interiors.

_____

_____

Create a credit for superior acoustics in an office environment. What performance would have to be achieved to be eligible for an ID credit? What are some possible implementation strategies?

CREDIT	REQUIREMENT

THINK ABOUT IT

Investigate a couple of LEED projects in your area or in the USGBC case studies and see which ID points they earned.

INVESTIGATE

Find out the significant environmental factors that affect the design of commercial interiors projects in your region. Talk to design and construction professionals with the relevant experience or seek information through your USGBC chapter.

ASK AROUND

1 A project team is interested in pursuing bonus credit under the Regional Priority section. How can the team identify the credits that have been assigned additional weighting for the project's region?

    a) Submit a Credit Interpretation Request.

    b) Consult the local USGBC chapter.

    c) Refer to the USGBC website.

    d) There is no method to identify regionally significant credits.

3 As a rule of thumb, Innovation in Design credits for exemplary performance are awarded for _____. (Select two.)

    a) Reaching a 100% threshold.

    b) Doubling the credit requirements.

    c) Achieving the next incremental threshold.

    d) Demonstrating significant environmental benefit.

2 A LEED interiors project is pursuing an Innovation credit for exemplary performance of SS Credit 3.1: Alternative Transportation – Public Transportation Access. The project team is attempting this credit based on a transportation management plan. How must the plan function to demonstrate exemplary performance? (Select three.)

    a) It must be provided to all employees upon hire.

    b) It must be comprehensive in nature.

    c) It must quantify the anticipated reduction in automobile use.

    d) It must be posted in all employee break rooms and in areas visible to visitors.

    e) It must identify multiple transportation alternatives.

4 Which of the following would disqualify a strategy from qualifying for ID Credit 1: Innovation in Design as an innovative strategy? (Select two.)

    a) The strategy is not cost-effective.

    b) The approach addresses only part of the LEED project.

    c) The environmental benefit cannot be quantified.

    d) The concept requires ongoing analysis and/or maintenance.

    e) The methodology is applicable only to certain geographical locations.

5

A project team has multiple LEED APs serving on the project, including the design architect, urban ecologist, and lighting designer. How does this support the design integration required by LEED?

a) LEED AP status is required to access LEED Online.

b) The LEED AP completes the LEED Submittal Templates.

c) The LEED AP has a demonstrated understanding of the LEED rating system.

d) The LEED AP can answer Credit Interpretation Requests from the project team.

See Answer Key on page 202.

PRACTICE QUESTION ANSWER KEY

SUSTAINABLE SITES
PRACTICE QUESTION ANSWERS

1) **A, C.** Proximity to basic services is recognized under SS Credit 2: Development Density and Community Connectivity, and proximity to mass transit is recognized under SS Credit 3.1: Alternative Transportation – Public Transportation Access. Proximity to local organic farms and bicycle paths is not recognized within LEED for Commercial Interiors.

2) **C.** One method to achieve this credit allows a combination approach (high SRI and vegetated roof areas), which is solved for this project as follows:

(Area of Roof Meeting Minimum SRI * 1.33) + (Area of Vegetated Roof * 2) ≥ Total Roof Area.

The SRI of the roof is 69, which meets the SRI requirement for steep-sloped roof areas, but not low-sloped roof areas. Therefore, 6,000 square feet (60% of the total roof area) is compliant roof area. Plugging this into the equation:

(6,000 sf * 1.33) + (Area of Vegetated Roof * 2) ≥ 10,000 sf

Further reducing the equation:

8,000 sf + (Area of Vegetated Roof * 2) ≥ 10,000 sf

Further reducing the equation:

Area of Vegetated Roof * 2 ≥ 2,000 sf

Solving the equation:

Area of Vegetated Roof ≥ 1,000 sf

There is 2,000 square feet of flat roof area (20% of 10,000 sf), and of this area 1,000 square feet must be vegetated. So 50% (1,000 sf / 2,000 sf) of the flat roof area must be vegetated to comply with the credit requirements.

3) **A, C.** Only certain biofuels are recognized as eligible to qualify as renewable energy. Animal waste and landfill gas are allowable, while municipal solid waste is not. Additionally, while clean wood is permitted, wood contaminated with paints, halogens, arsenic, and other chemicals is not allowed. Finally, geo-exchange systems (geothermal or ground-source heat pumps) are earth-coupled HVAC applications that use vapor compression for heat transfer. These systems do not obtain significant quantities of deep-earth heat compared with geothermal electric systems, and are ineligible as a renewable energy system.

4) **D.** Projects must provide secure bicycle racks and/or storage for 5% of peak occupants. Shower and changing facilities must be provided for 0.5% of FTE. All required quantities are rounded up, so five bicycle spaces are required in addition to one shower.

5) **C.** Light trespass is defined as a component of light pollution that is emitted horizontally onto adjacent properties (as contrasted with sky glow, which is light pollution emitted up). Fixture shielding, while potentially contributing to sky glow control, is primarily purposed to address light trespass.

WATER EFFICIENCY
PRACTICE QUESTION ANSWERS

1) **A.** Lavatories for public use have a baseline of 0.5 gallons per minute. This flow rate is established by the Universal Plumbing Code (UPC) and International Plumbing Code (IPC) and goes beyond the EPAct 1992 baseline requirements.

2) **A, C, E.** The use of innovative wastewater technologies reduces wastewater generation and potable water demand while increasing local aquifer recharge.

3) **D.** Wastewater from toilets and urinals is always considered blackwater.

4) **B, D.** Increasing irrigation efficiency and designing the site landscaping for a low landscape coefficient are acceptable methods to reduce the

landscape water use per the LEED calculation methodology. The landscaped area must remain the same in both the baseline and design calculations, and the use of groundwater is considered equivalent to the use of potable water for the purposes of this credit.

5) **D.** The water use reduction credit calculations are based on occupancy. Therefore, while the project remains eligible to attempt this credit, the flush and flow rates of the base building fixtures must be used for this credit. Since these values were not identified, additional information is required to determine compliance.

ENERGY AND ATMOSPHERE PRACTICE QUESTION ANSWERS

1) **B.** Decreasing the lighting power density reduces heat gain to space, thereby reducing the need to offset these gains with mechanical cooling.

2) **A.** The International Performance Measurement and Verification Protocol (IPMVP) Volume I, Concepts and Options for Determining Energy and Water Savings, has been established by EVO and is the referenced standard for EA Credit 3, Measurement and Verification.

3) **A, B.** The mechanical plans should list the location and function of HVAC system automatic controls or sensors. Additionally, identification of thermal comfort control zones is required to confirm appropriate zoning.

4) **B.** Two points are available to projects that use submetering to measure and record energy uses within the tenant space, and the remaining three points are available when the tenant pays his or her own energy costs.

5) **C.** Once the owner's project requirements (OPR) are documented, the design team develops its basis of design (BOD) documentation to form the foundation for the commissioning process. The submittal review and design review(s) are to be conducted against the OPR and BOD to ensure that the design intent is maintained. The functional testing takes place once the systems are installed and operational, and the systems manual is delivered after completion of functional testing.

MATERIALS & RESOURCES PRACTICE QUESTION ANSWERS

1) **E.** The door can contribute toward MR Credit 4, Recycled Content, due to its preconsumer recycled content, and toward MR Credit 7, Certified Wood, due to its FSC certification. It is not eligible for MR Credit 5, Regional Materials, as manufacture must take place within 500 miles of the project site.

2) **A, C.** Finished ceilings, floors, and walls, as well as interior doors and built-in case goods, contribute toward credit achievement. Exterior windows, structural elements (such as wall framing), and equipment do not contribute.

3) **B.** Of the 10 tons of waste, 2 tons are soils that are excluded from consideration under this credit, for a total eligible waste of 8 tons. The 2 tons that were landfilled, as well as the 2 tons that were incinerated (regardless of their use for energy generation), are considered nondiverted. Therefore, 4 tons of the 8 tons were diverted, for a final diversion rate of 50%.

4) **D.** This prerequisite requires collection and storage of paper, corrugated cardboard, glass, plastic, and metal. While it is advisable to collect all recyclable materials, only these five are specifically required by LEED.

5) **C.** The credit requirements define rapidly renewable as materials that are typically harvested within a 10-year or shorter cycle.

INDOOR ENVIRONMENTAL QUALITY PRACTICE QUESTION ANSWERS

1) **D.** IAQ testing must be completed after construction is complete and before occupancy.

2) **B.** Furniture and seating may be GREENGUARD Indoor Air Quality certified.

3) **A, C.** Energy use is directly affected by the amount of outside air that is delivered to the space. Energy is generally required to move the air through the building (fan energy) as well as to maintain comfortable temperatures and humidity (HVAC energy). The need for increased ventilation should be balanced with the need to reduce overall energy use.

4) **B.** A VOC budget calculation is allowable for projects that intentionally or unintentionally use products that exceed the established threshold for the specific application. Since the quantity applied is small, and the VOC levels are only slightly exceeded, it is likely that the VOC budget calculation will yield compliant results.

5) **A.** Smoking must be prohibited within 25 feet of all building entrances, operable windows, and air intakes. Additionally, signage must be posted to allow smoking in designated areas, prohibit smoking in designated areas, or prohibit smoking on the entire property.

INNOVATION IN DESIGN & REGIONAL PRIORITY PRACTICE QUESTION ANSWERS

1) **C.** Regional priority credits are listed on the USGBC website.

2) **B, C, E.** Exemplary performance is often granted for reaching the next incremental threshold, although this credit allows project teams to achieve exemplary performance by implementing a comprehensive transportation management plan.

Properly executed transportation management plans are comprehensive in nature (addressing all the ways occupants typically commute), quantify the anticipated reduction in automobile use, and identify as many alternatives as possible.

3) **B, C.** Exemplary performance credits are awarded for exceeding the threshold, in a significant way, of existing LEED credits. The established thresholds for each credit's exemplary performance are listed in the reference guide, although the general rule is that the levels are either doubled or in line with a consistent progression of incremental thresholds.

4) **B, C.** Innovative strategy credits must be comprehensive in nature, applicable to other projects, significantly better than standard sustainable design practices, and quantifiable.

5) **C.** LEED AP status is not required to complete the LEED Submittal Templates or to access LEED Online. Additionally, only USGBC can answer Credit Interpretation Requests. The LEED AP, in passing the professional accreditation exam, has demonstrated a level of understanding of USGBC and LEED, and therefore serves as a valuable resource to project teams pursuing LEED certification.

ACRONYMS AND ORGANIZATIONS

ANSI	American National Standards Institute
AP	LEED Accredited Professional
APPA	Association of Physical Plant Administrators
ASHRAE	American Society of Heating, Refrigerating and Air-Conditioning Engineers
CFC	Chlorofluorocarbon
cfm	cubic feet per minute
CIR	Credit Interpretation Request
COC	Chain of Custody
CRI	The Carpet and Rug Institute
DHW	Domestic hot water
DOE	U.S. Department of Energy
EA	Energy and Atmosphere category
EER	Energy Efficiency Rating
EPA	U.S. Environmental Protection Agency
ET	Evapotranspiration
FSC	Forest Stewardship Council
GBCI	Green Building Certification Institute
GHGs	Greenhouse Gases
gpf	gallons per flush
gpm	gallons per minute
GS	Green Seal
HCFC	Hydrochlorofluorocarbon
HEPA	Eigh-Efficiency Particle Absorbing
HVAC	Heating, Ventilation and Air Conditioning
Hz	Hertz
IAP	ENERGY STAR with Indoor Air Package
IAQ	indoor air quality
IEQ	Indoor Environmental Quality category
IESNA	Illuminating Engineering Society of North America

IPC	International Plumbing Code
kW	kilowatt
kWh	kilowatt-hour
LED	Light-Emitting Diode
LEED	Leadership in Energy and Environmental Design
MERV	Minimum Efficiency Reporting Value
MR	Materials and Resources category
SEER	Seasonal Energy Efficiency Rating
SHGC	Solar Heat Gain Coefficient
SMACNA	Sheet Metal and Air Conditioning Contractors' National Association
SRI	Solar Reflectance Index
SS	Sustainable Sites category
UPC	Uniform Plumbing Code
USGBC	U.S. Green Building Council
VOC	Volatile Organic Compound
WE	Water Efficiency category

CREDIT REVIEW SHEET

Test your knowledge of individual credits. Make several printed copies of this sheet, then fill in the blanks from memory for each credit you want to practice.

CATEGORY: _____ NUMBER: _____ AVAILABLE POINTS: _____

NAME: _____

EXEMPLARY PERFORMANCE: _____

TIME LINE: _____ TEAM: _____

INTENT:

_____

_____

REQUIREMENTS:

_____

_____

IMPLEMENTATION STRATEGIES:

_____

_____

REFERENCED STANDARDS:

_____

_____

RELATED CREDITS:

_____

_____

DOCUMENTATION & CALCULATIONS:

_____

_____

EQUATIONS:

_____

_____

ADDITIONAL NOTES:

_____

_____

KEY TERMS:

_____

_____

EXEMPLARY PERFORMANCE MATRIX

SUSTAINABLE SITES		
CREDIT	**EXEMPLARY PERFORMANCE ELIGIBILITY**	**THRESHOLD**
SS Credit I: Site Selection, Option 2: PATH 4: Heat Island Effect – Nonroof	Projects may earn credit for exemplary performance under SS Credit 1, Path 12, Other Quantifiable Environmental Performance, by demonstrating that two or more of the compliance paths described above have been met.	2 or more compliance paths
SS Credit I: Site Selection, Option 2: PATH 5: Heat Island Effect – Roof	Projects may earn credit for exemplary performance under SS Credit 1, Path 12, Other Quantifiable Environmental Performance, by demonstrating that 100% of the building's roof area (excluding mechanical equipment, photovoltaic panels, and skylights) consists of a vegetated roof system.	100%
SS Credit 1: Option 2: PATH 10: Water Use Reduction	Projects may earn an exemplary performance credit under SS Credit 1, Path 12, Other Quantifiable Environmental Performance, by demonstrating a 40% water use reduction for the whole building.	40%
SS Credit 1: Option 2: PATH 11: On-site Renewable Energy	Projects may earn an exemplary performance credit under SS Credit 1, Path 12, Other Quantifiable Environmental Performance, by demonstrating that on-site renewable energy accounts for 10% or more of the annual building energy cost.	10%

WATER EFFICIENCY		
CREDIT	**EXEMPLARY PERFORMANCE ELIGIBILITY**	**THRESHOLD**
WE Credit 1: Water Use Reduction	Projects may earn an innovation point for exemplary performance by demonstrating 45% reduction in projected potable water use.	45%

ENERGY AND ATMOSPHERE		
CREDIT	**EXEMPLARY PERFORMANCE ELIGIBILITY**	**THRESHOLD**
EA Credit 1.1: Optimize Energy Performance – Lighting Power	Project teams may earn an exemplary performance point by reducing the lighting power density 40% or more below the standard.	40%
EA Credit 1.2: Optimize Energy Performance – Lighting Controls	Project teams may earn an exemplary performance point by implementing daylight-responsive controls for 75% of the connected lighting load or by installing occupancy-responsive controls for 95% of the connected lighting load.	75%
EA Credit 1.3: Optimize Energy Performance – HVAC	Projects that use Option 2 and demonstrate that HVAC system component performance for the tenant space is 33% more efficient than a system that is in minimum compliance with ASHRAE 90.1–2007 are eligible to earn 1 point under Innovation in Design.	33%
EA Credit 1.4: Optimize Energy Performance – Equipment and Appliances	Projects may earn an exemplary performance credit under Innovation in Design by achieving a rated power of 97% attributable to ENERGY STAR–qualified equipment and appliances.	97%
EA Credit 4: Green Power	Project teams may earn an Innovation in Design point for exemplary performance by meeting 100% of the calculated annual use (or a default of 16 kWh per square foot per year) through contracted green power.	100% or a default of 16 kWh

MATERIALS AND RESOURCES

CREDIT	EXEMPLARY PERFORMANCE ELIGIBILITY	THRESHOLD
MR Credit 1.2: Building Reuse – Maintain Interior Nonstructural Components	Project teams may earn an Innovation in Design credit for exemplary performance by reusing 80% or more of the existing walls, flooring, and ceiling systems.	80%
MR Credit 2: Construction Waste Management	Project teams may earn an Innovation in Design credit for exemplary performance by diverting 95% or more of total construction waste.	95%
MR Credit 3.1: Materials Reuse	Project teams may earn an Innovation in Design credit for exemplary performance if the value of salvaged or reused materials used on the project is 15% or more of the total materials cost.	15%
MR Credit 3.2: Materials Reuse – Furniture and Furnishings	Project teams may earn an Innovation in Design credit for exemplary performance by using at least 60% salvaged, refurbished, or reused furniture and furnishings.	60%
MR Credit 4: Recycled Content	Project teams may earn an Innovation in Design credit for exemplary performance by achieving a total recycled-content value of 30% or more.	30%
MR Credit 5: Regional Materials	Project teams may earn an Innovation in Design credit for exemplary performance by achieving a total value of regionally harvested, extracted, and manufactured materials of 20% or more.	20%
MR Credit 6: Rapidly Renewable Materials	Project teams may earn an Innovation in Design credit for exemplary performance by achieving a rapidly renewable materials content of 10% or more.	10%
MR Credit 7: Certified Wood	Project teams may earn an Innovation in Design credit for exemplary performance by achieving an FSC-certified wood content of 95% or more of the project's total new wood.	95%

INDOOR ENVIRONMENTAL QUALITY

CREDIT	EXEMPLARY PERFORMANCE ELIGIBILITY	THRESHOLD
IEQ Credit 8.2: Daylight and Views – Views for Seated Spaces	Exemplary performance may be demonstrated for this credit by meeting two of the four following measures: 1. 90% or more of regularly occupied spaces have multiple lines of sight to vision glazing in different directions at least 90 degrees apart. 2. 90% or more of regularly occupied spaces have views that include views of at least two of the following: 1) vegetation, 2) human activity, or 3) objects at least 70 feet from the exterior of the glazing. 3. 90% or more of regularly occupied spaces have access to unobstructed views located within the distance of three times the head height of the vision glazing. 4. 90% or more of regularly occupied spaces have access to views with a view factor of 3 or greater, per the Heschong Mahone Group study, Windows and Offices; A Study of Office Worker Performance and the Indoor Environment, page 47, for their primary view (seated at workstation, facing computer screen). See: http://h-m-g.com/downloads/Daylighting/day_registration_form.htm to download the report at no charge.	2 of 4 measures

REFERENCE STANDARD TABLE

REFERENCE TITLE	REFERENCE DESCRIPTION	WEBSITE
American National Standards Institute (ANSI)/ASHRAE 52.2–1999, Method of Testing General	Ventilation Air-Cleaning Devices for Removal Efficiency by Particle Size This standard presents methods for testing air cleaners for 2 performance characteristics: the device's capacity for removing particles from the air stream and the device's resistance to airflow. The minimum efficiency reporting value (MERV) is based on 3 composite average particle size removal efficiency points. Consult the standard for a complete explanation of MERV calculations.	http://www.ashrae.org
American National Standards Institute (ANSI)/ ASHRAE Standard 55–2004: Thermal Environmental Conditions for Human Occupancy	ASHRAE 55–2004 identifies the factors of thermal comfort and the process for developing comfort criteria for a building space and its occupants. ASHRAE states, "This standard specifies the combinations of indoor space environment and personal factors that will produce thermal environmental conditions acceptable to 80% or more of the occupants within a space. The environmental factors addressed are temperature, thermal radiation, humidity, and air speed; the personal factors are those of activity and clothing."	http://www.ashrae.org
American National Standards Institute (ANSI)/Sheet Metal and Air Conditioning Contractors' National Association (SMACNA) 008–2008, IAQ Guidelines for Occupied Buildings under Construction, 2nd edition, 2007	The Sheet Metal and Air Conditioning Contractors National Association (SMACNA) is an international organization that developed guidelines for maintaining healthful indoor air quality during demolitions, renovations, and construction. The full document covers air pollutant sources, control measures, IAQ process management, quality control and documentation, interpersonal communication , sample projects, tables, references, resources, and checklists.	http://www.smacna.org
American National Standards Institute ANSI–E779–03, Standard Test Method for Determining Air Leakage Rate by Fan Pressurization	This test method covers a standardized technique for measuring air leakage rates through a building envelope under controlled pressurization and depressurization; it should produce a measurement of the air tightness of a building envelope.	http://www.astm.org.
ANSI/ASHRAE/IESNA Standard 90.1-2007, Energy Standard for Buildings Except Low-Rise Residential Buildings	American Society of Heating, Refrigerating and Air-Conditioning Engineers American National Standards Institute. American Society of Heating, Refrigerating and Air-Conditioning Engineers Illuminating Engineering Society of North America ANSI/ASHRAE/IESNA 90.1–2007 was formulated by ASHRAE under an ANSI consensus process. IESNA is a joint sponsor of the standard. ANSI/ASHRAE/IESNA 90.1–2007 establishes minimum requirements for the energy-efficient design of buildings, with these exceptions: single-family houses; multifamily structures of 3 habitable stories or fewer above grade; manufactured houses (mobile and modular homes); buildings that do not use either electricity or fossil fuel; and equipment and portions of buildings systems that use energy primarily for industrial, manufacturing, or commercial processes. Building envelope requirements are provided for semiheated spaces, such as warehouses. The standard provides criteria in the general categories shown in Table 1. Within each section are mandatory provisions and additional prescriptive requirements. Some sections also contain a performance alternative. The energy cost budget method (Section 11) allows the project team to exceed some of the prescriptive requirements, provided energy cost savings are made in other areas. However, in all cases, the mandatory provisions must still be met.	http://www.ashrae.org

REFERENCE TITLE	REFERENCE DESCRIPTION	WEBSITE
ASTM D1003–07E1,Standard Test Method for Haze and Luminous Transmittance of Transparent Plastics	This test method covers the evaluation of specific light-transmitting and wide-angle-light-scattering properties of planar sections of materials such as essentially transparent plastic.	http://www.astm.org
ASTM E1903-97, Phase II Environmental Site Assessment, effective 2002	A Phase II environmental site assessment is an investigation that collects original samples of soil, groundwater, or building materials to analyze for quantitative values of various contaminants. This investigation is normally undertaken when a Phase I assessment has determined a potential for site contamination. The substances most frequently tested are petroleum hydrocarbons, heavy metals, pesticides, solvents, asbestos, and mold.	http://www.astm.org
ASTM E1980–01, Standard Practice for Calculating Solar Reflectance Index of Horizontal and Low-Sloped Opaque Surfaces	This standard describes how surface reflectivity and emissivity are combined to calculate a solar reflectance index (SRI) for a roofing material or other surface. The standard also describes a laboratory and field testing protocol that can be used to determine SRI.	http://www.astm.org
ASTM E408–71(1996)e1, Standard Test Methods for Total Normal Emittance of Surfaces Using Inspection-Meter Techniques	This standard describes how to measure total normal emittance of surfaces using a portable inspection-meter instrument. The test methods are intended for large surfaces where nondestructive testing is required. See the standard for testing steps and a discussion of thermal emittance theory.	http://www.astm.org
ASTM E903–96, Standard Test Method for Solar Absorptance, Reflectance, and Transmittance of Materials Using Integrating Spheres	Referenced in the ENERGY STAR roofing standard, this test method uses spectrophotometers and need be applied only for initial reflectance measurement. It specifies methods of computing solarweighted properties using the measured spectral values. This test method is applicable to materials having both specular and diffuse optical properties. Except for transmitting sheet materials that are heterogeneous, patterned, or corrugated, this test method is preferred over Test Method E1084. The ENERGY STAR roofing standard also allows the use of reflectometers to measure roofing materials' solar reflectance. See the roofing standard for more details.	http://www.astm.org
ASTM International	ASTM International develops international standards for materials, products, systems and services used in construction, manufacturing and transportation.	http://www.astm.org
California Low Rise Residential Alternative Calculation Method Approval Manual, Home Energy Rating Systems (HERS)	Required Verification and Diagnostic Testing, California Energy Commission	http://www.energy.ca.gov/HERS/%20
Carpet and Rug Institute (CRI) Green Label Plus Testing Program	The Carpet and Rug Institute (CRI) is a trade organization representing the carpet and rug industry. Green Label Plus is an independent testing program that identifies carpets with very low VOC emissions. The CRI website describes the program and the associated VOC emission criteria in micrograms per square meter per hour. These criteria were developed by the Carpet and Rug Institute (CRI) in coordination with California's Sustainable Building Task Force and the California Department of Health Services (DHS).	http://www.carpet-rug.com

REFERENCE TITLE	REFERENCE DESCRIPTION	WEBSITE
	In the CRI Green Label Plus Program, emission rates must be verified by annual tests. Approved certification numbers can be reviewed on the CRI website under Indoor Air Quality/Green Label Plus/Approved companies. Approved products are listed under the company heading.	
Center for Resource Solutions, Green-e Renewable Electricity Certification Program	Green-e Energy is a voluntary certification and verification program for renewable energy products. Green-e certifies products that meet environmental and consumer protection standards developed in conjunction with environmental, energy, and policy organizations. Sellers of Green-e–certified energy must disclose clear and useful information to customers. Three types of renewable energy options are eligible for Green-e certification: renewable energy certificates, utility green-pricing programs, and competitive electricity products. The Green-e standard that went into effect on January 1, 2007, supersedes previous regional and product-specific criteria. Products exhibiting the Green-e logo are greener and cleaner than the average retail electricity product sold in that particular region. To be eligible for the Green-e logo, companies must meet certain criteria. The first criterion is the inclusion of qualified sources of renewable energy content such as solar electric, wind, geothermal, biomass, and small or certified low-impact hydro facilities. Other criteria are the inclusion of new renewable energy content (to support new generation capacity); compliance with emissions regulations for the nonrenewable portion of the energy product; and the absence of nuclear power. Companies must also meet other criteria regarding renewable portfolio standards. Criteria are often specific to a state or region of the United States. Refer to the standard for more details.	http://www. green-e.org (888) 634-7336
Chartered Institute of Building Services Engineers (CIBSE) Applications Manual 10, Natural Ventilation in Non-Domestic Buildings, 2005	CIBSE Applications Manual 10 provides guidance for implementing natural ventilation in nonresidential buildings. It provides detailed information on how to adopt natural ventilation as the sole servicing strategy for a building or as an element in a mixed mode design. According to the publisher, this manual "is a major revision of the Applications Manual (AM) first published in 1997. At the time, there was a significant expansion of interest in the application of engineered natural ventilation to the design of non-domestic buildings. The original AM10 sought to capture the state of knowledge as it existed in the mid-90s and present it in a form suited to the needs of every member of the design team. Some 10 years on from the time when the initial manual was conceived, the state of knowledge has increased, and experience in the design and operation of naturally ventilated buildings has grown. This revision of AM10 is therefore a timely opportunity to update and enhance the guidance offered to designers and users of naturally ventilated buildings."	http://www.cibse. org/
ENERGY STAR®– Qualified Products	Products in more than 50 categories are eligible for ENERGY STAR certification. They use less energy, save money, and help protect the environment.	http://www. energystar.gov
Environmental Technology Verification (ETV) Large Chamber Test Protocol for Measuring Emissions of VOCs and Aldehydes, effective September 1999	Under the leadership of the EPA, a testing protocol committee developed the referenced standards. The protocol requires the placement of the seating product or furniture assembly to be tested in a climatically controlled chamberA controlled quantity of conditioned air is drawn through the chamber, and emission concentrations are measured at set intervals over a 4-day period.	http://www. epa.gov/etv/ pdfs/vp/07_vp_ furniture.pdf

REFERENCE TITLE	REFERENCE DESCRIPTION	WEBSITE
FloorScore™ Program	According to its website, "The FloorScore program, developed by the Resilient Floor Covering Institute (RFCI) in conjunction with Scientific Certification Systems (SCS), tests and certifies flooring products for compliance with indoor air quality emission requirements adopted in California. Flooring products include vinyl, linoleum, laminate flooring, wood flooring, ceramic flooring, rubber flooring, wall base, and associated sundries." Carpet Testing Criteria: Carpet must not exceed the maximum target emission factors used in the CRI Green Label program and follow the test protocol used by Green Label Plus. Test results submitted must be no more than 2 years old at the time of submission. Standard Practice for the Testing of Volatile Organic Emissions from Various Sources using Small-Scale Environmental Chambers (State of California Specification Section 01350).	http://www.rfci.com/int_FloorScore.htm
Forest Stewardship Council's Principles and Criteria	Certification by the Forest Stewardship Council (FSC) is a seal of approval awarded to forest managers who adopt environmentally and socially responsible forest management practices, and to companies that manufacture and sell products made from certified wood. This seal enables consumers, including architects and specifiers, to identify and procure wood products from well-managed sources and thereby use their purchasing power to influence and reward improved forest management activities around the world. LEED accepts certification according to the comprehensive system established by the internationally recognized Forest Stewardship Council. FSC was created in 1993 to establish international forest management standards, known as the FSC principles and criteria, to ensure that forestry practices are environmentally responsible, socially beneficial, and economically viable. These principles and criteria are also intended to ensure the long-term health and productivity of forests for timber production, wildlife habitat, clean air and water supplies, climate stabilization, spiritual renewal, and social benefit, such as lasting community employment derived from stable forestry operations. These global principles and criteria are translated into meaningful standards at a local level through region-specific standard-setting processes. FSC also accredits and monitors certification organizations. The certifiers are independent, thirdparty auditors that are qualified to annually evaluate compliance with FSC standards on the ground and to award certifications. There are 2 types of certification: • Forest management certification is awarded to responsible forest managers after their operations successfully complete audits of forestry practices and plans. • Chain-of-custody (COC) certification is awarded to companies that process, manufacture, and/or sell products made of certified wood and who successfully complete audits to ensure proper use of the FSC name and logo, segregation of certified and noncertified materials in manufacturing and distribution systems, and observation of other relevant FSC rules (e.g., meeting minimum requirements for FSC fiber content in assembled and composite wood products). The majority of FSC certification audits performed in North America are conducted by SmartWood and Scientific Certification Systems (SCS), which are based in the United States. A limited number are performed by SGS, which is based in Europe.	http://www.fscus.org

REFERENCE TITLE	REFERENCE DESCRIPTION	WEBSITE
Green Seal Standard 36 (GS–36), effective October 19, 2000	Green Seal is an independent, nonprofit organization that strives to achieve a healthier and clean erenvironment by identifying and promoting products and services that cause less toxic pollution and waste, conserve resources and habitats, and minimize global warming and ozone depletion. GS–36 sets VOC limits for commercial adhesives. Green Seal Standard for Commercial Adhesives GS–36 requirements went in effect on October 19, 2000.	http://www.greenseal.org/certification/standards/commercial_adhesives_GS_36.cfm
Green Seal Standard GC–03	GC–03 sets VOC limits for anti-corrosive and anti-rust paints. Chemical Component Limitations— VOC: the manufacturer shall demonstrate that the paint is not formulated to exceed VOC concentrations.	http://www.greenseal.org/certification/standards/anti-corrosivepaints.pdf
Green Seal Standard GS–11	Green Seal is an independent nonprofit organization that strives to achieve a healthier and cleaner environment by identifying and promoting products and services that cause less toxic pollution and waste, conserve resources and habitats, and minimize global warming and ozone depletion. GS–11 sets VOC limits for commercial flat paints and nonflat paints . Tables 1 and 2 summarize Green Seal Standard GS–11.	www.greenseal.org/certification/standards/paints_and_coatings.pdf
GreenguardTM Certification Program	GEI has "established performance-based standards to define goods with low chemical and particle emissions for use indoors," primarily for building materials; interior furnishings; furniture; electronics; and cleaning, maintenance, and personal care products. The standard establishes certification procedures that include "test methods, allowable emissions levels, product sample collection and handling, testing type and frequency, and program applicaiton processes and acceptance."	http://www.greenguard.org
Hardcopy or microfiche (836 pages): National Technical Information Service (PB93-234672)	This document discusses a variety of management practices that can remove pollutants from stormwater volumes. Chapter 4, Part II, addresses urban runoff and suggests strategies for treating and filtering stormwater volumes after construction is completed.	http://www.epa.gov/OWOW and http://www.ntis.gov
Illuminating Engineers Society of North America	On-site renewable or site-recovered energy that might be used to achieve EA Credit 2, Enhanced Commissioning, is handled as a special case in the modeling process. If either renewable or recovered energy is produced at the site, the energy cost budget method considers it free energy and it is not included in the design energy cost. See the Calculation section for details.	
International Association of Plumbing and Mechanical Officials Uniform Plumbing Code	Section 402.0: Water-Conserving Fixtures and Fittings, effective 2006	
International Association of Plumbing and Mechanical Officials, Uniform Plumbing Code, Section 402.0, Water-Conserving Fixtures and Fittings, effective 2006 Publication IAPMO/ANSI UPC 1-2006.	The Uniform Plumbing Code defines water-conserving fixtures and fittings for water closets, urinals, and metered faucets. This ANSI-accredited code safeguards life, health, property, and public welfare by regulating and controlling the design, construction, installation, quality, location, operation, maintenance, and use of plumbing systems.	http://www.iapmo.org

REFERENCE TITLE	REFERENCE DESCRIPTION	WEBSITE
International Code Council	The International Plumbing Code defines maximum flow and consumption rates for plumbing fixtures and fittings for use in public and private lavatories, showerheads, sink faucets, urinals, and water closets.	http://www.iccsafe.org
International Code Council, International Plumbing Code, Section 604, Design of Building Water Distribution System, effective 2006	The International Plumbing Code defines maximum flow and consumption rates for plumbing fixtures and fittings for use in public and private lavatories, sink faucets, urinals, and water closets.	http://www.iccsafe.org
International Performance Measurement and Verification Protocol Volume I, Concepts and Options for Determining Energy and Water Savings, effective 2001	The Efficiency Valuation Organization is a nonprofit organization whose vision is a global marketplace that properly values energy and water efficiency. IPMVP Volume I defines basic terminology used in the measurement and verification field. It defines general procedures for achieving reliable and cost-effective determination of savings. Verification of actual savings is specific to each project. Volume I is written for general application in measuring and verifying the performance of projects that improve energy or water efficiency in buildings and industrial plants.	http://www.evo-world.org
International Standard ISO 14021–1999, Environmental Labels and Declarations, Self-Declared Environmental Claims (Type II Environmental Labeling)	International Organization for Standardization (ISO) This International Standard specifies requirements for self-declared environmental claims, regarding products, including statements, symbols and graphics for products. It further describes selected terms commonly used in environmental claims and gives qualifications for their use. It also describes a general evaluation and verification methodology for self-declared environmental claims and specific evaluation and verification methods for the selected claims.	http://www.iso.org
LEED Accredited Professional, Green Building Certification Institute	Individuals who successfully complete the LEED professional accreditation exam are LEED APs.Accreditation certifies that the individual has the knowledge and skills necessary to participate in the LEED application and certification process, holds a firm understanding of green building practices and principles, and is familiar with LEED requirements, resources, and processes. The Green Building Certification Institute (GBCI), established with the support of the U.S. Green Building Council (USGBC), handles exam development and delivery to ensure objective and balanced management of the credentialing program.	www.gbci.org
New Buildings Institute, Advanced Buildings™ Core Performance™ Guide	The Advanced Buildings program is a prescriptive plan for exceeding the energy performance requirements of ASHRAE 90.1–2004. It offers a predictable alternative to energy performance modeling and a simple set of criteria for significantly increasing building energy performance. The program updates and replaces the Advanced Buildings Benchmarked program. Core Performance is calibrated to exceed the requirements of ASHRAE 90.1–2004 in all climate zones. Information about the Core Performance program requirements and a range of additional reference material are available at http://www.advancedbuildings.net. Several aspects of the Core Performance program overlap with other LEED credits and prerequisites. Following the Core Performance program is not an alternative path to achieving any LEED credits except EA Credit 1.3, Optimize Energy Performance—HVAC, but Core Performance may facilitate earning other LEED credits and prerequisites.	http://www.advancedbuildings.net.

REFERENCE TITLE	REFERENCE DESCRIPTION	WEBSITE
Publication IAPMO/ ANSI UPC 1-2006	The Uniform Plumbing Code defines water-conserving fixtures and fittings for water closets, urinals, and metered faucets. This code, accredited by the American National Standards Institute, safeguards life, health, property, and public welfare by regulating and controlling the design, construction, installation, quality, location, operation, maintenance, and use of plumbing systems. International Code System, International Plumbing Code, Section 604, Design of Building Water Distribution System, effective 2006.	http://www. iapmo.org
South Coast Air Quality Management District (SCAQMD) Amendment to South Coast Rule 1168, VOC Limits, effective January 7, 2005	The South Coast Air Quality Management District is a governmental organization in southern California with the mission to maintain healthful air quality for its residents. The organization established source-specific standards to reduce air quality impacts.	http://www.aqmd. gov/rules/reg/ reg11/r1168.pdf
South Coast Air Quality Management District (SCAQMD) Rule 1113, Architectural Coatings	The South Coast Air Quality Management District is a governmental organization in southern California with the mission to maintain healthful air quality for its residents. The organization established source-specific standards to reduce air quality impacts.	http://www.aqmd. gov/rules
State of California Specification Section 01350	This standard practice document specifies carpet emissions testing criteria that will satisfy the credit requirements.	www.ciwmb. ca.gov/Green Building/specs/ Section 01350/#Indoor
The Carbon Trust Good Practice Guide 237, Natural Ventilation in Non-Domestic Buildings,	A Guide for Designers, Developers, and Owners, 1998 According to the Carbon Trust, "Carefully designed, naturally ventilated buildings can be cheaper to construct, maintain and operate than more heavily serviced equivalents. Occupants generally prefer windows that can be opened, and natural light, both of which are features of well designed, naturally ventilated buildings. The Guide summarizes the benefits of natural ventilation and considers the commercial implications, illustrating the issues by means of case studies."	To obtain a copy, search for "GPG 237" on the Carbon Trust Energy website or go to www. carbontrust. co.uk/ Publications/ publicationdetail. htm?productid=G PG237&metaNo Cache=1.
The Energy Policy Act (EPAct) of 1992 (and as amended)	This act addresses energy and water use in commercial, institutional, and residential facilities.	
The Energy Policy Act (EPAct) of 2005	This statute became U.S. law in August 2005. International Association of Plumbing and Mechanical Officials, Publication IAPMO/American National Standards Institute UPC 1–2006	
U.S. EPA 840B92002, Guidance Specifying Management Measures for Sources of Non-Point Pollution in Coastal Waters, effective January 1993	Many categories and subcategories of nonpoint sources could affect coastal waters and thus could potentially be addressed in this management measures guidance. Including all such sources in this guidance would have required more time than the tight statutory deadline allowed. For this reason, Congressman Studds stated in his floor statement, "The Conferees expect that EPA, in developing its guidance, will concentrate on the large nonpoint sources that are widely recognized as major contributors of water pollution."	http://www.epa. gov/owow/nps/ MMGI

REFERENCE TITLE	REFERENCE DESCRIPTION	WEBSITE
	This guidance thus focuses on five major categories of nonpoint sources that impair or threaten coastal waters nationally: (1) agricultural runoff; (2) urban runoff (including developing and developed areas); (3) silvicultural (forestry) runoff; (4) marinas and recreational boating; and (5) channelization and channel modification, dams, and streambank and shoreline erosion. EPA has also included management measures for wetlands, riparian areas, and vegetated treatment systems that apply generally to various categories of sources of nonpoint pollution.	
U.S. EPA Compendium of Methods for the Determination of Air Pollutants in Indoor Air	According to the Compendium, the EPA created this document to "provide regional, state and local environmental regulatory agencies with step-by-step sampling and analysis procedures for the determination of selected pollutants in indoor air. Determination of pollutants in indoor air is a complex task, primarily because of the wide variety of compounds of interest and the lack of standardized sampling and analysis procedures. The Compendium has been prepared to provide a standardized format for such analytical procedures. A core set of 10 chapters with each chapter containing 1 or more methods are presented in the current document. Compendium covers a variety of active and passive sampling procedures, as well as several analytical techniques both on and off site."	This standard is available from NTIS (800) 553-6847 with the ordering number PB90200288.
U.S. EPA Definition of Brownfields	The EPA Sustainable Redevelopment of Brownfields Program With certain legal exclusions and additions, brownfield site means real property, the expansion, redevelopment, or reuse of which may be complicated by the presence or potential presence of a hazardous substance, pollutant, or contaminant (Public Law 107-118, H.R. 2869, Small Business Liability Relief and Brownfields Revitalization Act). See the EPA website for additional information and resources.	http://www.epa.gov/brownfields
U.S. EPA's Environmental Technology Verification (ETV) Large Chamber Test Protocol for Measuring Emissions of VOCs and Aldehydes, effective September 1999	Under the leadership of the EPA, a testing protocol committee developed the referenced standards. The protocol requires the placement of the seating product or furniture assembly to be tested in a climatically controlled chamber. A controlled quantity of conditioned air is drawn through the chamber, and emission concentrations are measured at set intervals over a 4-day period.	http://www.epa.gov/nrmrl/std/etv/pubs/07_vp_furniture.pdf
Uniform Plumbing Code 2006, Section 402.0, Water-Conserving Fixtures and Fittings	UPC defines water-conserving fixtures and fittings for water closets, urinals, and metered faucets. This ANSI-accredited code safeguards life, health, property, and public welfare by regulating and controlling the design, construction, installation, materials, location, operation, and maintenance or use of plumbing systems.	http://www.iapmo.org

LEED 2009 for Commercial Interiors

Project Checklist

Project Name

Date

Sustainable Sites — Possible Points: 21

Y	N	?			
			Credit 1	Site Selection	1 to 5
			Credit 2	Development Density and Community Connectivity	6
			Credit 3.1	Alternative Transportation—Public Transportation Access	6
			Credit 3.2	Alternative Transportation—Bicycle Storage and Changing Rooms	2
			Credit 3.3	Alternative Transportation—Parking Availability	2

Water Efficiency — Possible Points: 11

Y	N	?			
Y			Prereq 1	Water Use Reduction—20% Reduction	
			Credit 1	Water Use Reduction	6 to 11

Energy and Atmosphere — Possible Points: 37

Y	N	?			
Y			Prereq 1	Fundamental Commissioning of Building Energy Systems	
Y			Prereq 2	Minimum Energy Performance	
Y			Prereq 3	Fundamental Refrigerant Management	
			Credit 1.1	Optimize Energy Performance—Lighting Power	1 to 5
			Credit 1.2	Optimize Energy Performance—Lighting Controls	1 to 3
			Credit 1.3	Optimize Energy Performance—HVAC	5 to 10
			Credit 1.4	Optimize Energy Performance—Equipment and Appliances	1 to 4
			Credit 2	Enhanced Commissioning	5
			Credit 3	Measurement and Verification	2 to 5
			Credit 4	Green Power	5

Materials and Resources — Possible Points: 14

Y	N	?			
Y			Prereq 1	Storage and Collection of Recyclables	
			Credit 1.1	Tenant Space—Long-Term Commitment	1
			Credit 1.2	Building Reuse	1 to 2
			Credit 2	Construction Waste Management	1 to 2
			Credit 3.1	Materials Reuse	1 to 2
			Credit 3.2	Materials Reuse—Furniture and Furnishings	1
			Credit 4	Recycled Content	1 to 2
			Credit 5	Regional Materials	1 to 2
			Credit 6	Rapidly Renewable Materials	1
			Credit 7	Certified Wood	1

Indoor Environmental Quality — Possible Points: 17

Y	N	?			
Y			Prereq 1	Minimum IAQ Performance	
Y			Prereq 2	Environmental Tobacco Smoke (ETS) Control	
			Credit 1	Outdoor Air Delivery Monitoring	1
			Credit 2	Increased Ventilation	1
			Credit 3.1	Construction IAQ Management Plan—During Construction	1
			Credit 3.2	Construction IAQ Management Plan—Before Occupancy	1
			Credit 4.1	Low-Emitting Materials—Adhesives and Sealants	1
			Credit 4.2	Low-Emitting Materials—Paints and Coatings	1
			Credit 4.3	Low-Emitting Materials—Flooring Systems	1
			Credit 4.4	Low-Emitting Materials—Composite Wood and Agrifiber Products	1
			Credit 4.5	Low-Emitting Materials—Systems Furniture and Seating	1
			Credit 5	Indoor Chemical & Pollutant Source Control	1
			Credit 6.1	Controllability of Systems—Lighting	1
			Credit 6.2	Controllability of Systems—Thermal Comfort	1
			Credit 7.1	Thermal Comfort—Design	1
			Credit 7.2	Thermal Comfort—Verification	1
			Credit 8.1	Daylight and Views—Daylight	1 to 2
			Credit 8.2	Daylight and Views—Views for Seated Spaces	1

Innovation and Design Process — Possible Points: 6

Y	N	?			
			Credit 1.1	Innovation in Design: Specific Title	1
			Credit 1.2	Innovation in Design: Specific Title	1
			Credit 1.3	Innovation in Design: Specific Title	1
			Credit 1.4	Innovation in Design: Specific Title	1
			Credit 1.5	Innovation in Design: Specific Title	1
			Credit 2	LEED Accredited Professional	1

Regional Priority Credits — Possible Points: 4

Y	N	?			
			Credit 1.1	Regional Priority: Specific Credit	1
			Credit 1.2	Regional Priority: Specific Credit	1
			Credit 1.3	Regional Priority: Specific Credit	1
			Credit 1.4	Regional Priority: Specific Credit	1

Total — Possible Points: 110

Certified 40 to 49 points   Silver 50 to 59 points   Gold 60 to 79 points   Platinum 80 to 110

USGBC LEED AP Interior Design + Construction Study Guide